RECIPE
REHAB

everyday HEALTH **with JoAnn Cianciulli and Maureen Namkoong, M.S., R.D.**

RECIPE
REHAB

80 DELICIOUS RECIPES
THAT SLASH THE FAT, NOT THE FLAVOR

HARPER WAVE

An Imprint of HarperCollins Publishers
www.harpercollins.com

FIRST EDITION

Food photographs by Ben Fink

Chef photographs by Vanessa Stump

Library of Congress Cataloging-in-Publication Data

Namkoong, Maureen.

Recipe rehab : 80 delicious recipes that slash the fat, not
the flavor / JoAnn Cianciulli and Maureen Namkoong,
M.S., R.D.—First edition.
    p.   cm
Includes index.
ISBN 978-0-06-227290-4
1. Diet therapy.   2. Reducing diets—Recipes.
3. Low-calorie diet—Recipes.   4. Celebrity chefs.
I. Cianciulli, JoAnn.   II. Title.
RM216.N27   2013
641.5'6384—dc23   2013004603

13 14 15 16 17   OV/RRD   10 9 8 7 6 5 4 3 2 1

Contents

Foreword

Candice Kumai

When I was asked to cook on the premiere season of what became the hit show *Recipe Rehab* on ABC stations, my initial reaction was; "Why hadn't anyone produced a show like this before!?" Finally, there was a TV program that shared not only a fresh perspective on delicious, satisfying meals created by real chefs, but also provided a huge wake-up call about the kinds of (un-healthy) foods we are feeding our families on a daily basis.

We've all heard the statistics about the health crisis facing Americans: About two-thirds of the adult population is classified as overweight or obese, and among our children, approximately one in three kids and teens is overweight or obese. Even more disturbing is the fact that, according to a recent study, the number of obese adults is on track to increase dramatically over the next twenty years. It's clear that this is a complex problem that will require a number of approaches to solve, from changes in public policy to changes in our attitudes and lifestyles. But one change we can all implement *right now* is to spend a little more of our time cooking and eating healthy meals at home.

It has been shown that shared family meals have a number of healthy benefits: families who cook at home and eat together are known to eat more fruits and vegetables, eat fewer fried foods and junk foods, and drink less soda than other families. And kids who eat at home with their families have a lower body mass index (BMI) than those who don't—they also perform better in school!

What I love about *Recipe Rehab* is that it gives everyone in America the power to create incredible-tasting, restaurant-quality foods *that are also good for them,* right in his or her own kitchen. Each week, two celebrity chefs face off in a competition to transform a family's favorite unhealthy, high-calorie dish into something that tastes just as delicious, but is much healthier. And when I say the chefs face off, I'm not kidding—we are in it to win it! Here's the lineup of my fierce competitors, whose recipes you will soon be preparing and eating (for more information on these amazing chefs, turn to page viii): Spike Mendelsohn, Aida Mollenkamp, Scott Leibfried, Govind Armstrong, Jet Tila, Jill Davie, Daniel Green, Laura Vitale, Calvin Harris, Jaden Hair, and Mareya Ibrahim.

We are lucky to have an amazingly talented group of notable chefs, food writers, and cooks on this show (as well as on RecipeRehab.com and in this book)! We've all signed on to be a part of the *Recipe Rehab* project because we care deeply about the health and wellness issues facing Americans. As culinary professionals, we feel that it is our duty to share the knowledge and skills we've learned in the kitchen through years of hard work and practice to help home cooks find "small step" solutions they can implement little by little, leading to big payoffs down the road for themselves and their families. With *Recipe Rehab*, we're able to give people the tools and information they need to create dishes they can feel good about cooking any night of the week.

We've also got you covered online—and on the go—with RecipeRehab.com. Inspired by the book, the site caters to anyone looking for easy, accessible ways to eat healthier. With tons of chef tips, simple swaps, how-to videos, and more, RecipeRehab.com makes it easier than ever for home cooks to get healthy without skipping all their favorite foods. We also believe that health should never be an inconvenience—breakfast on the go or last-minute weeknight dinners can be fast, delicious, and still good for the whole family.

All of the recipes in this book were created by real chefs and trained professionals who know a thing or two about how to make food taste delicious and look beautiful, and how to translate "chef-y" recipes into easy-to-master meals for anyone cooking at home.

For example, Chef Laura Vitale's French Toast Casserole is the perfect Sunday-morning breakfast for a crowd. It can be prepared the night before, so you just pop it in the oven in the morning and, voilà—a warm, wholesome breakfast for only 160 calories per serving. And then there's Chef Jill Davis's "Better than Takeout" Orange Chicken, an amazing weeknight dinner option that you can whip together in a mere thirty minutes (less time than it takes for your local Chinese joint to deliver!), and offers plenty of flavor and nutrition for under 500 calories. And of course, there's always room for dessert. Chef Spike Mendelsohn will show you how to make his flaky, delicious Phyllo Apple Cups, which take fifteen minutes to bake and will satisfy your apple pie cravings for less than 150 calories!

In addition to sharing our favorite recipes, we also wanted to empower you to make healthier versions of your own family traditions. Throughout the book you'll find tips and tricks that will help you get creative and rehab your favorite over-the-top recipes with improved cooking techniques and smart ingredient substitutions.

Being part of the *Recipe Rehab* TV show, Web site, and book has been a humbling and moving experience for me. I feel lucky to have met so many incredible people, and to have the opportunity to watch firsthand as families' lives are changed by the simple act of cooking the right foods, the right way. I urge you to take inspiration from those families and try, cook, test, taste, and explore all of the recipes in this book. And even more important, I urge you to get excited about eating real, delicious, clean foods again. Making better choices is in! Being healthy and happy will never go out of style.

Life should be full of good taste.

xx,

Meet Our Chefs . . .

 CHEF SPIKE MENDELSOHN is the owner of two Washington, D.C., restaurants, Good Stuff Eatery and We, The Pizza. He has cooked at the famed Les Crayères in France, worked for Thomas Keller at Bouchon in Napa Valley, and spent time at Le Cirque and Mai House in New York City. A familiar face to many TV viewers, Chef Spike competed on Bravo's *Top Chef Chicago* and Top *Chef All-Stars*, and the Food Network's *The Next Iron Chef*.

 CHEF AIDA MOLLENKAMP attended Cornell University's School of Hotel Administration and honed her kitchen skills at Le Cordon Bleu in Paris. She is the food editor at *CHOW* magazine and star of *FoodCrafters* on the Cooking Channel. She was previously the host of *Ask Aida* on the Food Network, and is the author of the cookbook *Keys to the Kitchen*.

 CHEF SCOTT LEIBFRIED has appeared on Gordon Ramsay's reality show *Hell's Kitchen* for the past ten seasons. He is also the lead chef adviser for the *Kitchen Nightmares* series. Chef Scott developed his passion for wholesome food from his family, who have been farming produce since the 1930s. He has worked at the Four Seasons Hotel restaurant in Beverly Hills, and is the executive chef for Napa Valley Grille in Westwood, California.

 CHEF GOVIND ARMSTRONG is the chef and co-owner of the acclaimed Table 8 Restaurants in Los Angeles and Miami as well as 8 oz. Burger Bar and Post & Beam, which is expanding to several cities nationwide. Chef Govind has worked under such legendary California-based chefs as Wolfgang Puck (at the original Spago in Los Angeles), and Mary Sue Milliken and Susan Feniger at City. He has appeared as a judge on *Top Chef*, and as a contestant on *Iron Chef America*.

 CHEF JET TILA began cooking at an early age, growing up in his family's Thai restaurant kitchens in Los Angeles. He served as the executive chef of Wazuzu, a pan-Asian bistro at on the Las Vegas strip, from 2008 to 2011, and most recently opened a new restaurant in Santa Monica, the Charleston.

CHEF JILL DAVIE is the chef de cuisine at Josie restaurant, named one of the top twenty-five restaurants in L.A. by *Los Angeles Magazine*. She was named one of the top ten students of the year at the Culinary Institute of America and received the "Baby Chef" from *Food and Wine* magazine. She's also competed on the Food Network's *The Next Iron Chef* and is the cohost of *Shopping with Chefs* on Fine Living TV with David Myers.

CHEF DANIEL GREEN hails from England and is author of three cookbooks, which feature health-conscious and delicious recipes. Inspired by his own successful weight loss, he advocates for healthy cooking, and has made television appearances on the BBC and many other networks.

CHEF LAURA VITALE is a chef, writer, and the host the popular YouTube cooking series, *Laura in the Kitchen*. Born and raised in Italy until the age of twelve, Laura learned the joy and art of Italian cooking from her grandmother, and later worked in her family's restaurants.

CHEF CALVIN HARRIS is an award-winning chef and renowned culinary developer who created the refrigerated meals for the Biggest Loser line of healthy meals. He most recently launched Inspired Food Solutions, which seeks to promote new, wholesome food brands.

CHEF JADEN HAIR is a recipe developer and food columnist with a passion for fast, fresh, and simple recipes. She is the publisher of SteamyKitchen.com, which was recently dubbed one of the best food blogs by *Forbes*. She is also a food columnist for Discovery Health and TLC and is the author of the *Steamy Kitchen Cookbook*.

CHEF MAREYA IBRAHIM is "the Fit Foody"—a chef, writer, educator, and award-winning food industry entrepreneur. Her mission is to help show how easy and satisfying it is to "make every bite count" with food that feeds your body, not just your face.

CANDICE KUMAI received her culinary training at Le Cordon Bleu California School of Culinary Arts and has cooked in several California-based restaurants. An alumnus of Bravo's *Top Chef*, season 1, Candice is currently a judge on the Food Network's *Iron Chef America*, and is the author of two cookbooks, *Cook Yourself Sexy* and *Pretty Delicious*. She also stars on the E! reality series *Playing with Fire*.

Pumpkin Pancakes with Spiced Apples, page 15

Part 1

POWER
BREAKFASTS

Grab-and-Go Bagel and Lox Sandwich

Breakfast sandwiches are more popular than ever, but that greasy bagel sandwich from the coffee shop or "muffin sandwich" from the drive-through is no way to start your morning. This grab-and-go favorite was rehabbed using bagel thins in place of bagels, which typically contains 500 or more calories and are the equivalent of five servings of bread! Made with fresh tomatoes and cucumber, cream cheese, and smoked salmon, this sandwich is nutritious and satisfying. If you're unable to find bagel thins at your grocery store, you can substitute whole grain English muffins.

MAKES 4 SANDWICHES

½ cup whipped cream cheese

1 tablespoon capers, drained and finely chopped

1 scallion, green part only, finely chopped

½ cup arugula or other bitter lettuce, such as watercress

Juice of ½ lemon

½ teaspoon fresh-ground black pepper

4 whole wheat bagel thins, halved and toasted

4 (1-ounce) slices smoked salmon

1 beefsteak tomato, sliced and patted dry

1 cucumber, unpeeled and sliced

¼ small red onion, thinly sliced

In a small bowl, combine the cream cheese, capers, and chopped scallion tops. Mix well with a fork to evenly blend the ingredients. In another small bowl, toss the arugula with the lemon juice and pepper.

To assemble, spread about 1 tablespoon of the caper cream cheese on the bottom half of each toasted bagel thin. Lay a slice of smoked salmon and tomato on top, followed by a few slices of cucumber and onion. Scatter the arugula across and top with the other half of the bagel to enclose. Cut in half and serve immediately.

Per serving: 294 calories, 11 g total fat (5 g saturated), 66 mg cholesterol, 336 mg sodium, 25 g protein, 6 g fiber, 29 g carb

Tropical Parfait

When you pick up a yogurt parfait at your local coffee shop, you probably think you're choosing a healthy breakfast. The truth is, while parfaits may look nutritious, there's a lot of sugar lurking in that convenient cup. The combination of fruit in a sugary syrup and clusters of sweetened granola can send your blood sugar soaring, which means you'll be starving again before lunchtime. But healthy parfaits are easy to make at home and take along in your own reusable plastic container. For a less fancy approach, skip the pretty layers and simply mix together the yogurt and fruit and top with low-fat granola and coconut.

MAKES 4 PARFAITS

2 cups cut fresh tropical fruit, such as pineapple, mango, papaya, or kiwi, or a mixture

2 cups nonfat vanilla Greek yogurt

2 cups Dried Fruit and Almond Granola (see page 10)

½ cup shredded unsweetened coconut, toasted

Using 4 juice glasses or mason jars, spoon ¼ cup of fruit into each glass, evening it out with the back of a tablespoon. Top with ¼ cup of the yogurt and ¼ cup of granola. Repeat the layering process one more time with the remaining fruit, yogurt, and granola. Top each parfait with 2 tablespoons of coconut before serving.

Per serving (1 parfait): 407 calories, 11 g total fat (6 g saturated), 0 mg cholesterol, 63 mg sodium, 20 g protein, 8 g fiber, 60 g carb

French Toast Casserole with Blueberry Syrup

Recipe by Chef Laura Vitale

In the French Toast Challenge, Chef Laura squared off against Chef Jill to re-create an indulgent breakfast favorite. Before Chef Laura's rehab, this recipe bore more of a resemblance to dessert than to breakfast. Chef Laura swapped out white bread for whole wheat and replaced whole eggs and whole milk with egg whites and almond milk, providing protein and calcium while trimming fat and calories. This baked casserole is perfect for weekend brunch—just prep it the night before, refrigerate, and pop it in the oven the next morning.

SERVES 8

FRENCH TOAST:

Nonstick cooking spray

16 slices "light" wheat bread, crust removed, slightly stale, and cut into 1-inch pieces

3 cups unsweetened vanilla almond milk

2 large eggs

2 large egg whites

3 tablespoons stevia sugar substitute, such as Truvia

Finely grated zest of ½ orange (1 teaspoon)

2 teaspoons pure vanilla extract

2 teaspoons ground cinnamon

pinch teaspoon salt

SYRUP:

2 cups fresh or frozen blueberries

Juice of 1 orange (¼ cup)

2 tablespoons maple syrup

2 tablespoons water

To make the French toast, coat an 8-by–8-inch baking dish with nonstick spray. Arrange the bread in the dish and set aside.

In a large bowl, mix together the almond milk, eggs, egg whites, stevia, zest, vanilla, cinnamon, and salt.

Pour the egg mixture over the bread cubes. Allow bread cubes to soak for at least 10 minutes, and up to overnight. (Cover and place in refrigerator if soaking more than 1 hour.)

When ready to bake, preheat the oven to 400°F. Cover the baking dish with aluminum foil. Bake until the bread is slightly puffed, about 30 minutes. Remove the foil and continue to bake until the top is golden and crusty, about 10 minutes. Remove from oven and allow to stand for a few minutes before serving.

To make the blueberry syrup, combine the blueberries, orange juice, maple syrup, and water in a small saucepan over medium heat. Cook and stir until the berries break down, about 5 minutes.

Serve the French toast topped with a spoonful of the blueberry sauce, the remainder of the sauce on the side.

> **REHAB TIP: BLUEBERRIES**
> These powerful little berries contain high levels of immune-boosting anti-oxidants, which work to neutralize free radicals in the body. A one-cup serving has just 80 calories and provides 25 percent of your daily recommendation for vitamin C. If fresh berries aren't in season, you can always use frozen.

Per serving: 160 calories, 3 g total fat (< 1 g saturated), 47 mg cholesterol, 377 mg sodium, 7 g protein, 9 g fiber, 29 g carb

Stuffed French Toast with "No-Tella"

Recipe by Chef Jill Davie

This luscious dish was Chef Jill's answer to the French Toast Challenge. In addition to rehabbing French toast, this recipe also rehabs another favorite indulgence: chocolate hazelnut spread. The traditional jarred version you'll find in grocery stores contains more calories, fat, and sugar than chocolate frosting! Substituting almond butter for hazelnuts is a great way to keep the nutty flavor, and when you mix it with unsweetened cocoa powder, agave, and nonfat yogurt, you get "no-tella," a fine substitute for the rich Italian spread.

SERVES 4

NO-TELLA:

¼ cup almond butter

2 tablespoons unsweetened cocoa powder

3 tablespoons agave nectar

2 tablespoons nonfat plain yogurt

FRENCH TOAST:

1 cup sweetened vanilla almond milk

4 large egg whites

1 teaspoon ground cinnamon

¼ teaspoon ground allspice

¼ teaspoon ground nutmeg

1 tablespoon light agave nectar

1 (8-ounce) whole wheat baguette, cut on the diagonal into ½-inch slices

Nonstick cooking spray

TOPPING:

2 cups stemmed and sliced strawberries

Juice of ½ lemon

1 teaspoon light brown sugar

To make the no-tella, in a mixing bowl combine the almond butter, cocoa, and agave nectar. Stir with a spoon until smooth. Stir in the yogurt. Set aside.

To make the French toast, in a mixing bowl whisk together the almond milk, egg whites, cinnamon, allspice, nutmeg, and agave nectar until foamy.

Spread 2 tablespoons of the no-tella on one half of the bread slices. Place the remaining bread on top of these slices to create sandwiches.

Coat a frying pan with nonstick cooking spray and place over medium-high heat. Submerge the no-tella sandwiches into the egg mixture. Shake off any extra liquid and place sandwiches into the pan.

Working in batches, brown the bread until crisp and golden, 3 to 4 minutes. Brown the other side until the outside is crisp and golden and the inside of the French toast is gooey and hot, about 2 minutes.

To make the topping, in a medium bowl toss the strawberries with the lemon juice and brown sugar.

To serve, cut the French toast into thirds and arrange among four plates. Scatter the sliced strawberries evenly on top and serve with any extra no-tella on the side.

REHAB TIP: ALMOND BUTTER
Almond butter, made by crushing and smoothing almonds into a thick paste, is a rich, delicious alternative to peanut butter. Almonds are higher in calcium and fiber than peanuts, and while they do contain a high amount of fat, it is mostly heart-healthy, unsaturated fat.

Per serving: 365 calories, 11 g total fat (<1 g saturated), 0 mg cholesterol, 447 mg sodium, 14 g protein, 8 g fiber, 59 g carb

Dried Fruit and Almond Granola

Made with dried fruit and nuts, this granola takes all of 15 minutes to throw together and get into the oven, and it contains a lot less sugar than what you'll find at the grocery store. Granola can be stored in an airtight container for up to two weeks.

MAKES 12 SERVINGS

4 cups rolled oats (not instant)

½ cup wheat germ

¼ cup ground flaxseed (meal)

½ cup mixed dried fruit, such as dates, apricots, and bananas, coarsely chopped if necessary

3 tablespoons slivered almonds

1 tablespoon light brown sugar

1 teaspoon ground ginger

½ teaspoon ground cinnamon

½ cup thawed frozen concentrated apple juice

2 tablespoons honey or agave nectar

2 tablespoons maple syrup

1 tablespoon pure vanilla extract

Preheat the oven to 300 degrees F.

In a mixing bowl, combine the oats, wheat germ, flaxseed, dried fruit, and almonds. Sprinkle with the sugar, ginger, and cinnamon. Toss with your hands to evenly distribute the ingredients.

In a microwave-safe bowl, combine the apple juice, honey or agave nectar, maple syrup, and vanilla. Microwave on high, uncovered, for 1 minute. (If you don't have a microwave, combine the ingredients in a small pot over medium-low heat until hot.)

Drizzle the hot syrup over the dry ingredients. Toss well until fully coated.

Spread the mixture in an even layer in a baking pan. Bake for 45 minutes, shaking the pan from time to time to crisp the granola evenly.

Let the granola cool for about 10 minutes to reach room temperature. Note: When you first take the granola out of the oven, it will feel a little soft to the touch; it becomes crispy as it cools.

Per serving (½ cup): 217 calories, 4 g total fat (< 1 g saturated), 0 mg cholesterol, 11 mg sodium, 7 g protein, 5 g fiber, 38 g carb

Chef Tip: Flaxseed

Similar to sesame seeds in size and shape, flax has a nutty flavor and sturdy texture. Flaxseed is a good source of omega-3 fats, fiber, and antioxidants. To reap the full health benefits of flax, grind the seeds yourself in a coffee grinder or purchase ground flax meal.

Cheesy Broccoli and Potato Scramble

A big breakfast scramble is a quick and easy way to feed the whole family on a busy morning, and it provides a great opportunity to incorporate more vegetables into your day. Here, egg substitute is combined with broccoli, potatoes, and cheese, but you could also use red peppers, asparagus, tomatoes, or any other fresh vegetables you have on hand. At fewer than 300 calories per serving, this scramble starts your day with a nice balance of protein and carbs that will keep you energized all morning long.

SERVES 4

2 small red potatoes (about ½ pound), washed and cut into small cubes

¾ cup water

1 cup chopped broccoli florets, fresh or frozen and thawed (about ¼ pound)

1 tablespoon vegetable oil

2 garlic cloves, minced

¼ teaspoon red pepper flakes

2 cups liquid egg substitute, such as Egg Beaters

½ cup reduced-fat shredded cheddar cheese

2 teaspoons chopped fresh dill

4 slices multigrain bread, toasted, for serving

Put a deep skillet over medium-high heat. When the pan is hot, add the potatoes and water. Once the water comes to a boil, reduce the heat to medium-low and cover the pan with a lid or aluminum foil. Steam until the potatoes begin to soften, about 4 minutes. Add the broccoli, stirring to combine with the potatoes, and cover. Cook for 4 more minutes, until both vegetables are just fork tender. Drain the vegetables in a colander, wipe out the pan with a paper towel, and return to medium-high heat.

Coat the skillet with the oil. When the oil is hot, add the cooked broccoli, potato, garlic, and red pepper flakes. Cook and stir until the vegetables begin to brown on the edges, about 2 minutes. Pour in the egg substitute. Using a rubber spatula, drag the eggs from the outside of the pan to the center to create fluffy curds.

When the eggs are just about set, sprinkle in the cheese and dill. Remove the pan from the heat. Divide the scramble onto four plates with 1 piece of toast on each.

Per serving: 266 calories, 8 g total fat (2 g saturated), 10 mg cholesterol, 496 mg sodium, 21 g protein, 4 g fiber, 29 g carb

Chef Tip: Shredded Cheese

When shredding cheese, try to shred it as finely as possible—a finer grate creates more volume, so you can sprinkle a dish liberally using less cheese. For hard cheeses, a microplane achieves a very fine grate. Before grating softer cheeses, pop them in the freezer for 10 minutes: they'll firm up and be easier to work with.

Lemon Poppy Seed Muffins

Lemon poppy seed muffins are a delicious morning treat but are typically loaded with heavy fats like butter and oil. This rehabbed version replaces unhealthy fats with mashed banana, low-fat buttermilk, and egg whites. If you're storing the muffins for any longer than one day, line the bottom of a plastic container with paper towels. Place the muffins side by side (don't stack), then top with another layer of paper towels before sealing with the lid. The paper towels will absorb the extra moisture, and the muffins will retain their texture and flavor.

MAKES 12 MUFFINS

1 cup whole wheat flour

¾ cup all-purpose flour

2 teaspoons baking powder

1 teaspoon baking soda

1 cup sugar

½ teaspoon salt

¾ cup low-fat buttermilk

1 large ripe banana, mashed with a fork

3 large egg whites

Juice and finely grated zest of 2 lemons (about ½ cup juice and 1 tablespoon zest)

½ teaspoon pure almond extract

1 tablespoon poppy seeds

Preheat the oven to 375°F. Line a standard 12-capacity muffin pan with paper liners or coat with nonstick cooking spray.

In a mixing bowl, combine the flours, baking powder, baking soda, sugar, and salt. In a separate large bowl, combine the mashed banana and egg whites. Using a handheld electric mixer, beat the banana, buttermilk, and egg whites on medium speed until blended, about 1 minute. Add the lemon juice, zest, almond extract, and poppy seeds. Continue to beat until the mixture is smooth.

Reduce the mixer speed to low. Gradually add the dry ingredients, scraping down the sides of the bowl. Beat until the batter comes together and there are no visible lumps.

Using a ladle, pour the batter into the prepared pan, using about ¾ cup of batter per muffin cup. Bake for 30 minutes, until the muffins mound slightly and are firm to the touch. Allow muffins to cool in the pan for 10 minutes before removing.

Per serving: 155 calories, 1 g total fat (0 g saturated), 1 mg cholesterol, 314 mg sodium, 4 g protein, 2 g fiber, 35 g carb

REHAB TIP: FRUIT PUREES A typical store-bought muffin can start your day off with more than 600 calories and 25 grams of fat. Make your own delicious and healthy muffins at home, using fruit purees like mashed bananas, dates, or applesauce to add moisture and a touch of sweetness without a lot of added sugar and zero fat. Unsweetened applesauce is a terrific, easy substitute for butter or oil in many baking recipes.

Pumpkin Pancakes with Spiced Apples

Recipe by Chef Candice Kumai

The original version of this family favorite clocked in at more than 600 calories per serving. Chef Candice cut the calories and upped the nutritional value by using agave nectar in place of refined white sugar, reducing the butter, and adding canned pumpkin, which gives these pancakes moisture and richness. If you're cooking pancakes over the weekend, make some extra apple topping to mix with oatmeal or nonfat yogurt for quick breakfasts during the week.

MAKES 12 PANCAKES

SPICED APPLES:

1 tablespoon unsalted butter

2 Fuji apples, halved, cored, and thinly sliced

2 tablespoons dried currants or raisins

½ teaspoon pumpkin pie spice

1 tablespoon agave nectar

PANCAKES:

2 cups all-purpose flour

¼ cup agave nectar

2 teaspoons baking powder

2 teaspoons pumpkin pie spice

½ teaspoon salt

¾ cup canned pumpkin puree (not pumpkin pie filling)

3 large eggs

½ cup unsweetened applesauce

⅔ cup plain unsweetened almond milk

Nonstick cooking spray

½ cup nonfat plain Greek yogurt, for serving

To make the apple topping, melt the butter in a skillet over medium-low heat. Add the sliced apples and currants and cook until the apples are soft, about 15 minutes. Add the pumpkin pie spice and agave nectar. Cook and stir for about 5 more minutes. Remove from the heat, cover, and keep warm.

To make the pancakes, in a large mixing bowl whisk together the flour, baking powder, pumpkin pie spice, and salt. In a separate bowl, whisk the pumpkin puree, eggs, applesauce, agave nectar, and almond milk until well blended. Add the pumpkin mixture to the dry ingredients and stir until well combined. The batter will be thick.

Put a large nonstick griddle over medium heat and coat with cooking spray. Pour dollops of batter onto griddle, making three pancakes at a time. When the outer edges firm up, flip and cook the other side until golden brown, about a minute. Transfer the pancakes to a plate as they finish.

Serve two pancakes on each plate, topped with a spoonful of spiced apples and a dollop of Greek yogurt.

To watch a how-to video for this recipe, check out www.RecipeRehab.com.

Per serving: 331 calories, 5 g total fat (2 g saturated), 98 mg cholesterol, 389 mg sodium, 10 g protein, 4 g fiber, 63 g carb

Cranberry-Ginger Oatmeal

You already know what a difference a bowl of oatmeal makes: it warms you up, fills you up, and pumps you up like no other breakfast food. Some packaged instant oatmeal is full of sugar and artificial flavors. This healthy and delicious recipe uses real rolled oats that are toasted and then cooked in apple juice diluted with water. These small steps add flavor to the oatmeal and eliminate the need for added sugar.

SERVES 2

1 tablespoon unsalted butter

1 cup rolled oats (not instant)

1 cup unfiltered 100 percent natural apple juice

1 cup water

2 teaspoons peeled and grated fresh ginger

½ teaspoon ground cinnamon

¼ cup dried cranberries

Pinch salt

½ teaspoon pure vanilla extract

1 small banana, sliced, for serving

Put a pot over medium heat and add the butter. When the butter is melted, add the oats. Cook, stirring, until the oats are fragrant and toasted, about 2 minutes.

Pour the apple juice and water into the pot; stir in the ginger and cinnamon. Simmer gently for 5 minutes, until almost all of the liquid is absorbed and the oatmeal has thickened. Stir in the cranberries, salt, and vanilla and continue to cook until the oatmeal is tender and creamy and the cranberries soften, 3 to 5 minutes. Serve the oatmeal topped with the banana.

Per serving (1 cup): 379 calories, 9 g total fat (4 g saturated), 15 mg cholesterol, 151 mg sodium, 8 g protein, 7 g fiber, 70 g carb

Whole Grain Waffles with Ricotta

These light, crisp, not-too-sweet waffles are made with cornmeal and whole wheat flour, which lends them a slightly nutty flavor. Creamy ricotta cheese and lowfat buttermilk stand in for butter, producing waffles that are airy and moist. A warm drizzle of orange-infused honey is the perfect topping for this satisfying breakfast, which won't leave you feeling like you're on carb overload.

MAKES 8 WAFFLES

BATTER:

1½ cups whole wheat flour

½ cup cornmeal

2 tablespoons light brown sugar

1 teaspoon baking powder

½ teaspoon baking soda

1 teaspoon ground cinnamon

¼ teaspoon salt

1½ cups low-fat buttermilk

½ cup part-skim ricotta

2 large eggs, lightly beaten

1 tablespoon canola oil

2 teaspoons pure vanilla extract

2 teaspoons finely grated orange zest

Nonstick cooking spray

SYRUP:

¼ cup freshly squeezed orange juice

3 tablespoons honey

To make the waffles, in a mixing bowl combine the flour, cornmeal, sugar, baking powder, baking soda, cinnamon, and salt. In a separate bowl, whisk together the buttermilk, ricotta, eggs, oil, vanilla, and orange zest. Add the wet ingredients into the dry ingredients, mixing with a rubber spatula until well combined.

Heat a waffle iron according to manufacturer's instructions. Coat the surface with nonstick cooking spray.

While the waffle iron is heating, in a small bowl mix the orange juice with the honey. Heat the mixture in the microwave on high for 30 seconds.

Add enough batter to fill the holes of the waffle iron about three-quarters full (about ⅓ cup of batter). Close the waffle iron and cook until the waffles are crisp and golden brown, 3 to 4 minutes. Remove the waffles to a side plate and repeat with the remaining batter.

Place 2 waffles on each plate and drizzle with the orange-honey syrup. Serve immediately.

Per serving: 454 calories, 11 g total fat (3 g saturated), 106 mg cholesterol, 600 mg sodium, 17 g protein, 6 g fiber, 74 g carb

Chef Tip: Whole Wheat Flour

Whole wheat flour, which includes the wheat's bran, germ, and endosperm, is a must-have for a healthy pantry. Whole wheat flour has essential nutrients that have been stripped away from all-purpose white flour. One cup of whole wheat flour has 12 grams of fiber, as opposed to just 3 grams in white flour. Including more fiber in your diet can help lower cholesterol, control blood sugar, and aid in achieving a healthy weight.

Fully Loaded Breakfast Burritos with Avocado Salsa

Recipe by Chef Govind Armstrong

Breakfast burritos are a weakness for many people, especially if you live out West—they're available on seemingly every street corner! While those versions are typically packed with saturated fat and cholesterol, this rehabbed version cuts back on the unhealthy fat and increases the protein and fiber for a hearty, satisfying breakfast. Stuffed with eggs, black beans, grilled chicken, spinach, and low-fat cheddar cheese, this burrito really is fully loaded—with nutrition. For breakfast on the go, just add a spoonful of the salsa inside the burrito, wrap it in foil, and hit the road.

SERVES 6

AVOCADO SALSA:

2 plum (Roma) tomatoes, chopped

1 small ripe Hass avocado, halved, pitted, peeled, and cubed

4 scallions, white and green parts, chopped

½ cup fresh cilantro leaves, chopped

Juice of 1 lime

¼ teaspoon red pepper flakes

BURRITO:

1 tablespoon olive oil

1 red bell pepper, halved, cored, and thinly sliced

1 large onion, halved and thinly sliced

2 garlic cloves, sliced

½ cup canned black beans, drained and rinsed

1 tablespoon smoked paprika

¼ teaspoon coarse salt

¼ teaspoon freshly ground black pepper

2 cups baby spinach leaves

2 large eggs, preferably cage-free, lightly beaten

1 cup liquid egg substitute, such as Egg Beaters

1 cup reduced-fat shredded cheddar cheese

6 (6-inch) whole wheat tortillas, warm

12 ounces grilled skinless, boneless chicken breast, cut into small cubes

To make the salsa, in a mixing bowl combine the tomatoes, avocado, scallions, cilantro, lime juice, and red pepper flakes. Toss gently to coat, taking care not to smash the avocado. Lay a piece of plastic directly on the surface of the salsa to prevent the avocados from browning, and put in the refrigerator.

To make the burrito, place a large nonstick skillet over medium-high heat and coat with 1½ teaspoons of the oil. When the oil is hot, add the pepper, onion, and garlic. Cook and stir for 2 minutes or until soft. Add the beans to the pan and cook until they're heated through and there is no liquid remaining in the pan. Season the bean mixture with the smoked paprika, salt, and pepper. Add the spinach leaves, a handful at a time, folding the leaves over until wilted. Once all the spinach is incorporated, scrape the mixture into a bowl and cover to keep warm. Wipe out the skillet with a paper towel and return to medium heat.

Coat the skillet with the remaining 1½ teaspoons of oil. When the oil is hot, add the beaten whole eggs and egg substitute. Using a rubber spatula, gently stir the eggs until soft-scrambled, about 3 minutes. Sprinkle in the cheese and remove from the heat. Cover the skillet with a lid or aluminum foil to help the cheese melt into the eggs.

To assemble each burrito, divide the bean-and-vegetable mixture in the center of each tortilla, then scatter a few pieces of chicken on top, and finally the cheesy eggs. Fold the bottom of the tortilla up over the filling, tuck in the side flaps, and roll the burrito up over itself to enclose the filling. Serve the burritos with the avocado salsa on top.

To watch a how-to video for this recipe, check out www.RecipeRehab.com.

Per serving: 370 calories, 14 g total fat (4 g saturated), 124 mg cholesterol, 615 mg sodium, 34 g protein, 15 g fiber, 28 g carb

Chef Tip: Spinach

Low in calories and high in vitamins, spinach is one of the healthiest foods on the planet. It's a concentrated source of antioxidants, calcium, and vitamin A—which promotes healthy skin and even combats wrinkles! Fresh or frozen, add this nutritious green to your menu as often as possible.

Caramelized Onion, Bacon, and Mushroom Frittata

A frittata is a classic Italian egg dish, similar to an omelet but typically baked in the oven. While they can be a healthy choice, frittatas are often loaded with fat. This frittata rehab uses just two slices of bacon to provide all of the fat needed to sauté the vegetables, and the addition of egg whites gives it a light, soufflé-like texture. Sweet, caramelized onions and earthy mushrooms are combined with fresh herbs for the filling, while the addition of just a little goat cheese gives the dish a luscious, rich feel. Another great thing about this breakfast: You don't need to turn on the oven! The frittata cooks quickly on the stovetop.

SERVES 4

2 slices bacon

1 large onion, finely chopped

1 (8-ounce) package cremini mushrooms, wiped clean, stemmed, and sliced (about 2 cups)

2 garlic cloves, minced

2 teaspoons fresh thyme leaves, chopped

1 teaspoon fresh rosemary leaves, finely chopped

½ teaspoon freshly ground black pepper

6 large egg whites (about ¾ cup)

3 large eggs

¼ cup crumbled goat cheese

4 fresh chives, chopped

Place a 12-inch nonstick skillet over medium heat. When the pan is hot, add the bacon. Cook the bacon until crisp, about 5 minutes, then remove to a paper-towel-lined plate to drain, keeping the drippings in thepan. Put the onion in the skillet and cook, stirring, until it softens and begins to brown, about 5 minutes. Add the mushrooms, garlic, thyme, rosemary, and pepper. Continue to cook and stir until the mushrooms release their moisture, about 5 minutes.

In a separate bowl, whisk the egg whites and whole eggs until frothy. Pour the egg mixture into the skillet, making sure to spread out the mushroom-and-onion mixture so it will be evenly distributed in the frittata. Cook until the eggs are partially set, without stirring, about 5 minutes.

Sprinkle the cheese and chives evenly over the top of the frittata. Cover the pan with a lid, until the cheese softens and the eggs firm up, about 5 minutes. Crumble the bacon on top and cut into wedges.

Per serving: 176 calories, 10 g total fat (4 g saturated), 150 mg cholesterol, 266 mg sodium, 14 g protein, 1 g fiber, 7 g carb

REHAB TIP: EGG WHITES Nearly all of the fat and cholesterol in eggs are contained in the yolks, while the whites are basically pure protein. It is easiest to separate yolks from whites when eggs are cold. You can store leftover egg whites in a tightly sealed container in the refrigerator for up to one week, or frozen for a month. A good way to freeze egg whites is to put them in ice cube trays—simply pop out the cubes and add to recipes as needed.

Pita Nachos with Mango Salsa, page 31

Part 2

SIMPLE
STARTERS

Creamy Kale and Artichoke Dip with Garlic Toasts

Who can resist dipping into a bowl of warm, creamy artichoke dip? This popular appetizer seems healthy, but it's usually loaded with mayonnaise and cheese. This rehabbed version uses a mixture of part-skim ricotta and reduced-fat cream cheese to achieve the same creamy texture with a fraction of the fat and calories. Spinach is also swapped out in favor of kale, which has a chewier texture that can hold up to all of the moisture, as well as a nice peppery kick.

SERVES 12 (MAKES 6 CUPS)

DIP:

2 tablespoons olive oil

1 large onion, finely chopped

1 (12-ounce) bag frozen quartered artichoke hearts (about 3½ cups), thawed

½ (16-ounce) bag frozen chopped kale (about 3 cups), thawed

4 garlic cloves, minced

Juice of ½ lemon

¼ teaspoon kosher salt

¼ teaspoon red pepper flakes

½ (8-ounce) package reduced-fat cream cheese, at room temperature and cut into chunks

½ cup part-skim ricotta cheese

¾ cup finely grated Pecorino Romano or Parmesan cheese

GARLIC TOAST:

Nonstick cooking spray

1 (8-ounce) baguette, cut on the diagonal into ½-inch slices

2 garlic cloves, halved lengthwise

To make the dip, preheat the oven to 350°F. Put a large skillet over medium-high heat and coat with the oil. When the oil is hot, add the onion and artichoke hearts. Cook and stir until the vegetables begin to soften, about 6 to 8 minutes. Add the kale. Cook and stir until it loses its moisture, 3 to 4 minutes. Stir in the garlic, lemon juice, salt, and red pepper flakes; cook until fragrant, about 2 minutes. Remove the pan from the heat.

In a mixing bowl, stir together the cream cheese, ricotta, and ½ cup of the Pecorino. Add the vegetables to the cream cheese mixture and stir until combined. Scrape the mixture into a casserole dish and top with the remaining ¼ cup of Pecorino. Bake until the dip is bubbly and the cheese is melted, about 15 minutes.

To make the garlic toasts, coat a baking pan with nonstick cooking spray. Arrange the bread slices on the pan and spray the tops with cooking spray. Bake at 350°F for 8 to 10 minutes or until golden brown.

As soon as the toasts come out of the oven, quickly rub the cut side of the garlic over each piece once or twice.

Serve the hot dip with the garlic toasts.

Per serving: 167 calories, 7 g total fat (3 g saturated), 14 mg cholesterol, 334 mg sodium, 8 g protein, 3 g fiber, 19 g carb

Chef Tip: Kale

Kale is more popular than ever these days, and for good reason: Whether cooked or raw, it is a versatile ingredient that offers an incredible amount of nutrition for very few calories. Kale is packed with health-promoting sulfur compounds and is an excellent source of vitamins K, A, and C, as well as manganese, and is a very good source of calcium. When buying fresh kale, be sure to thoroughly wash and dry it before using.

Fresh Figs Wrapped in Prosciutto with Balsamic Glaze

It seems as though "bacon wrapped" everything is all the rage these days. One easy way to rehab a recipe that calls for bacon is to use prosciutto instead, which is sliced much thinner than bacon and contains less fat per serving. Here, sweet fresh figs are stuffed with a little blue cheese and then gently wrapped in a thin blanket of prosciutto for an elegant appetizer that will have your guests swooning. The balsamic glaze is worth the few extra minutes of prep time—it adds a real depth of flavor to this dish, and its rich color and smooth, shiny texture will make your presentation all the more seductive.

SERVES 6

FIGS:

12 fresh figs, either Black Mission or green Calimyrna (see tip, below)

1½ ounces blue cheese, crumbled into raisin-size pieces

6 thin slices prosciutto (3 ounces), cut lengthwise into 2 strips per slice

GLAZE:

½ cup balsamic vinegar

1 tablespoon honey

1 teaspoon freshly ground pepper

To make the figs, preheat the oven to 400°F.

Cut each fig in half lengthwise and stuff a raisin-size piece of blue cheese in the center. Wrap a strip of prosciutto around the fig, covering the cheese. Place the figs, cut side up, in a baking pan. Bake for 15 minutes, until the figs are soft and the prosciutto begins to crisp.

To make the glaze, pour the vinegar and honey into a small pot and put over medium-low heat. Gently simmer until the vinegar is reduced and syrupy, about 5 minutes. Stir in the pepper.

Serve the figs drizzled with the balsamic glaze.

Per serving (4 wrapped figs): 160 calories, 4 g total fat (2 g saturated), 16 mg cholesterol, 485 mg sodium, 7 g protein, 3 g fiber, 27 g carb

Chef Tip: Figs

Fresh figs are typically available in late summer through fall, and a real treat when in season. Figs are fragile and don't travel well, so if you see imperfect figs at the store, don't be alarmed--as long as they're not moldy or oozing liquid, they're probably perfectly fine. Try to eat or cook your figs within a few days of purchasing them, and avoid storing them in the refrigerator.

Grilled Sirloin Skewers with Homemade Steak Sauce

A lot of people avoid red meat for health reasons, but in moderation, red meat isn't such a bad thing. One of these skewers contains a whopping 28 grams of protein, for just over 200 calories. Top sirloin steak is a tender, moist cut of beef that's low in fat and has a deep, rich flavor.

SERVES 8

STEAK SAUCE:

1 teaspoon canola oil

1 small onion, coarsely chopped

2 garlic cloves, coarsely chopped

¼ cup fresh flat-leaf parsley, coarsely chopped

½ cup no-salt-added ketchup
½ cup low-sodium vegetable broth or water

1 tablespoon Worcestershire sauce

1 tablespoon instant coffee

1 teaspoon freshly ground black pepper

SKEWERS:

2 teaspoons paprika

1 teaspoon granulated onion

1 teaspoon granulated garlic

½ teaspoon ground mustard

½ teaspoon freshly ground black pepper

1½ pounds top sirloin steak, excess fat trimmed, cut into 1½-inch cubes

3 small zucchini, cut into 1-inch pieces

1 (8-ounce) package cremini mushrooms, stemmed and wiped of grit (about 16)

Nonstick cooking spray

½ teaspoon kosher salt

To make the steak sauce, put a small pot over medium heat and coat with the oil. Add the onion, garlic, and parsley; cook, stirring, for a couple of minutes to soften. Add the ketchup, broth, Worcestershire, coffee, and pepper. Reduce the heat to low, cover, and simmer for 15 minutes. Puree with an immersion blender or transfer to a standard blender. Set aside.

If using wooden skewers, submerge 8 skewers in a pan of water so that they have time to soak; this will keep them from burning on the grill pan.

In a small bowl, combine the paprika, onion, garlic, mustard, and black pepper. Put the cubed steak in a large bowl and add the spice blend, rubbing it into the meat. Cover and refrigerate for at least 30 minutes.

To assemble, thread a cube of beef onto the skewer first, followed by a piece of zucchini and a mushroom. Repeat this process, alternating the meat and vegetables to end with a piece of steak. You should have 3 beef cubes per skewer. Coat a grill pan with nonstick cooking spray and place over medium-high heat or preheat a gas or charcoal grill. Spray the steak skewers with cooking spray and season with salt. Grill the skewers, turning a few times, until the beef and vegetables are lightly charred on all sides and the meat is cooked to your liking, about 8 minutes. Serve the skewers with steak sauce on the side.

Per serving (1 skewer): 217 calories, 7 g total fat (2.5 g saturated), 76 mg cholesterol, 342 mg sodium, 27 g protein, 1 g fiber, 9 g carb

Spicy Sausage-Stuffed Mushrooms

Stuffed mushrooms are a cocktail-party classic. Oftentimes they're brimming with greasy bread crumbs and offer little in the way of nutrition or satiation. But these savory stuffed mushrooms are filled with a hearty mixture of spicy chicken sausage, feta cheese, and Japanese bread crumbs, which are lighter and flakier than traditional bread crumbs. Mushrooms make excellent little vehicles for stuffing—they're low in calories and packed with vitamins and minerals.

SERVES 4

Nonstick cooking spray

16 medium-size white or brown mushrooms, wiped clean (1 pound)

1 tablespoon olive oil

2 (2-ounce) links hot turkey sausage, such as Jennie-O® Lean Hot Italian Turkey Sausage, removed from casings

2 garlic cloves, minced

¼ cup Marsala or white wine

½ cup panko (Japanese-style bread crumbs)

½ cup crumbled feta cheese

2 tablespoons finely chopped fresh flat-leaf parsley

Pinch cayenne pepper, or to taste

¼ teaspoon kosher salt

¼ teaspoon freshly ground black pepper

Preheat the oven to 375°F. Spray a 9-by-13-inch baking dish with nonstick spray. Remove the stems from the mushrooms. Chop the stems finely and set aside.

Put a nonstick skillet over medium heat and coat with the oil. When the oil is hot, add the sausage, breaking it up with the back of a wooden spoon. Cook the sausage for 6 to 8 minutes, stirring frequently, until no longer pink. Add the chopped mushroom stems and garlic; cook and stir until the mushrooms lose their moisture and begin to brown, about 3 minutes. Stir in the wine and cook for 1 minute, until evaporated.

Add the bread crumbs, stirring to combine evenly with all of the other ingredients. Remove the pan from the heat. Add the feta, parsley, and cayenne, mixing well to incorporate. You should have about 2 cups.

Using a teaspoon, fill each mushroom cap with the sausage mixture, mounding it just above the top. Arrange the mushrooms in the baking dish and spray the tops with nonstick cooking spray. Season the mushrooms with salt and pepper.

Bake for 20 minutes, or until the mushrooms are tender and the stuffing is browned and crusty.

Per serving (4 mushrooms): 209 calories, 10 g total fat (4 g saturated), 35 mg cholesterol, 586 mg sodium, 11 g protein, 1 g fiber, 16 g carb

Chef Tip: Feta Cheese

Made from sheep's milk or goat milk, feta cheese is an excellent way to bring the tangy, salty flavor of cheese into a dish without adding a ton of fat and calories. Feta has about one-third less fat than hard cheeses, like cheddar, and has a strong flavor, so a little goes a long way.

Pita Nachos with Mango Salsa

Recipe by Chef Mareya Ibrahim

When Chef Mareya went head-to-head with Chef Laura in the Nacho Challenge, she decided to take the traditional dish in a whole new direction. Using a fresh mango-tomato salsa in place of traditional jarred salsa, and pita chips in place of tortilla chips, she created a sweet-spicy dish that's loaded with nutrients. The addition of grilled chicken adds a nice boost of protein, and makes these nachos filling and satisfying.

SERVES 6

MANGO-TOMATO SALSA:

1 ripe mango, halved, pitted, peeled, and diced (see tip, below)

2 medium tomatoes, finely chopped

½ medium red onion, finely chopped

1 jalapeño, halved, seeded if desired, and minced

2 garlic cloves, minced

3 tablespoons chopped fresh cilantro

Juice and finely grated zest of 1 lime

¼ teaspoon kosher salt

NACHOS:

6 pieces reduced-carb whole wheat pita bread, such as Joseph's

Nonstick cooking spray

2 teaspoons ground cumin

½ pound grilled skinless, boneless chicken breast, cubed

1 (15-ounce) can low-sodium black beans, drained and rinsed

2 cups reduced-fat shredded Monterey Jack cheese

1 cup nonfat plain Greek-style yogurt

Juice and finely grated zest of 1 lime

¼ teaspoon kosher salt

To prepare the salsa, in a mixing bowl combine the mango, tomato, onion, jalapeño, garlic, cilantro, lime juice, zest, and salt. Toss to mix the ingredients together. Set aside to allow the flavors to come together.

To prepare the nachos, preheat the oven to 300°F. Halve each pita bread horizontally, to separate the top and bottom half of the pita, to make 12 rounds. Cut each round into 8 wedges. Arrange the pita triangles in a single layer on two baking pans. Lightly spray the pita with nonstick cooking spray and sprinkle with cumin. Bake until very lightly crisp, about 5 minutes.

Top the toasted pita chips with the chicken and black beans and sprinkle on the cheese. Bake for 10 to 12 minutes or until cheese has melted.

In a small bowl, combine the yogurt, lime juice, zest, and salt. Set aside.

To serve: Put the nachos on a serving platter and top with dollops of the lime-yogurt sauce and a few spoonfuls of the salsa.

Per serving: 350 calories, 9 g total fat (5 g saturated), 41 mg cholesterol, 661 mg sodium, 28 g protein, 1 g fiber, 41 g carb

Chef Tip: Mangoes

The sweet, colorful flesh of mangoes makes for a vibrant salsa that is low in fat and full of flavor. A vitamin-C powerhouse, this well-loved tropical fruit packs a nutritional punch. One cup of fresh mango supplies 35 percent of your recommended daily allowance (RDA) of vitamin A and 100 percent of your RDA of vitamin C.

Nachos Supreme with Pico de Gallo

Recipe by Chef Laura Vitale

Most family nacho recipes are meant to re-create the indulgent plates served at restaurants and thus come loaded with cheese, refried beans, guacamole, and sour cream. Chef Laura's challenge was to rehab a family's nacho recipe that contained more than 800 calories and a day's worth of sodium per serving! Her lighter version retains that indulgent feeling, with Greek yogurt standing in for sour cream, black beans replacing refried beans, and low-fat cheese replacing the orange liquid stuff for total savings of 600 calories per serving.

SERVES 8

NACHOS:

4 cups baked, no-salt tortilla chips (about 4 ounces)

1 tablespoon olive oil

1 small onion, minced

2 garlic cloves, minced

1 (15-ounce) can black beans, drained and rinsed

2 teaspoons chili powder

½ teaspoon ground cumin

¾ cup reduced-fat shredded cheddar cheese

3 tablespoon pickled jalapeños, drained and chopped

¼ cup low-fat plain Greek-style yogurt

Zest of 1 lime, finely grated

Juice of ½ lime

½ teaspoon coarse salt

¼ teaspoon freshly ground black pepper

PICO DE GALLO SALSA:

3 plum (Roma) tomatoes, chopped

3 scallions, white and green parts, finely chopped

1 fresh jalapeño, halved, seeded, and finely chopped

¼ cup chopped fresh cilantro leaves

Juice of 1 lime

½ teaspoon coarse salt

¼ teaspoon freshly ground black pepper

Preheat the oven to 400°F. Put the tortilla chips in a large casserole dish and set aside.

Place a skillet or pot over medium heat and coat with the oil. When the oil is hot, add the onion and garlic. Cook and stir until the onion begins to soften, 3 to 4 minutes. Add the black beans, chili powder, and cumin. Cook and stir for another 3 to 4 minutes. Lightly mash the black beans with the back of a wooden spoon as they cook.

Spoon the black-bean mixture evenly over the chips and top with the cheese and pickled jalapeños. Bake until the cheese is melted, about 10 minutes. Meanwhile, in a small bowl, combine the yogurt with the lime zest and juice. Stir in salt and pepper and set aside.

To prepare the salsa, in a mixing bowl combine the tomatoes, scallions, jalapeño, cilantro, salt, and pepper. Using a slotted spoon to remove moisture, spoon salsa over baked chips. Top with dollops of yogurt and serve immediately.

Per serving: 157 calories, 6 g total fat (2 g saturated), 8 mg cholesterol, 564 mg sodium, 7 g protein, 5 g fiber, 23 g carb

Mini Crab Cakes with Mustard-Dill Sauce

Crab cakes are one of the most popular hors d'oeuvres out there, but most of the time they're made with a little crab and lots of fillers—plus they're fried, making them high in fat and calories. These baked crab cakes have a light, airy texture that allows the crabmeat to be the star of the show. To keep the sodium in check, no additional salt is added, so you can really taste the Old Bay and fresh lemon. A homemade mustard-dill sauce made with yogurt stands in for tartar sauce and adds a delicious, tangy note.

SERVES 4

1 tablespoon canola oil

2 scallions, white and green parts, finely chopped

2 garlic cloves, minced

1 jalapeño, halved, seeded, and finely chopped

16 ounces lump crabmeat, fresh or canned, drained and picked over for shells

¾ cup panko (Japanese-style bread crumbs)

2 tablespoons light mayonnaise

2 large egg whites, lightly beaten

1 teaspoon Dijon mustard

Juice and finely grated zest of 1 lemon

1 teaspoon Old Bay Seasoning

½ teaspoon freshly ground black pepper

Nonstick cooking spray

SAUCE:

¼ cup nonfat plain yogurt, either regular or Greek

1½ tablespoons Dijon mustard

1 tablespoon finely chopped fresh dill

Juice and finely grated zest of ½ lemon

To make the crab cakes, put a small skillet over medium heat and coat with the oil. When the oil is hot, add the scallions, garlic, and jalapeño. Cook and stir for 2 minutes, until soft and fragrant. Remove from the heat.

In a mixing bowl, combine the crabmeat, bread crumbs, mayonnaise, egg white, mustard, lemon juice, and zest. Scrape the scallion mixture into the bowl and season with the Old Bay and pepper. Fold together gently but thoroughly, taking care not to mash the crabmeat.

Using your hands, shape the mixture into 16 cakes, about 2 inches across and 1 inch thick. They should be moist and just hold together. Put the crab cakes on a plate, cover with plastic wrap, and refrigerate for at least 15 minutes (or up to one day) to firm them up.

Preheat the oven to 375°F. Coat a baking pan with nonstick cooking spray. Remove the crab cakes from the fridge and arrange side by side on the pan. Spray the tops with nonstick cooking spray.

Bake until the bottoms of the crab cakes are browned, about 15 minutes. Using a thin spatula or the tip of a knife, carefully flip the crab cakes over and return them to the oven for another 5 minutes, until the other side is golden.

To make the sauce, in a small bowl combine the yogurt, mustard, dill, lemon juice, and zest. Stir with a spoon until well blended.

Serve the crab cakes with the sauce drizzled over top.

Per serving (4 crab cakes): 240 calories, 7 g total fat (1 g saturated), 91 mg cholesterol, 770 mg sodium, 25 g protein, 1 g fiber, 17 g carb

Refried Bean Quesadilla with Guacamole Dipping Sauce

These crisp-on-the-outside, gooey-on-the-inside quesadillas give you all the cheesy goodness you crave, with about half the calories of most restaurant-style quesadillas. Sizzling peppers and onions give a nod to traditional fajitas and provide a nice charred flavor and texture, and the rich avocado dip allows you a touch of creamy indulgence without piling it on too thick. You could also serve this dip with vegetables or baked tortilla chips for a healthy appetizer or snack.

SERVES 8

GUACAMOLE DIPPING SAUCE:

- 1 ripe Hass avocado, halved, pitted, peeled, and coarsely chopped
- 1 cup frozen green peas, run under cool water to thaw
- ½ cup fresh cilantro, coarsely chopped
- 2 scallions, white and green parts, chopped
- 2 garlic cloves, smashed
- 1 jalapeño, halved, seeded if desired, and coarsely chopped
- Juice of 2 limes (about ¼ cup)
- 1 teaspoon ground cumin
- ½ teaspoon kosher salt
- ½ cup nonfat plain yogurt

QUESADILLAS:

- 1 tablespoon canola oil
- 1 poblano or small green bell pepper, halved, seeded, and thinly sliced
- ½ small red onion, thinly sliced
- ¼ cup water, plus more as needed
- 2 tablespoons tomato paste
- 1 teaspoon unsweetened cocoa powder
- 1 teaspoon dried oregano
- 1 (15-ounce) can pinto or kidney beans, drained and rinsed
- 8 (6-inch) whole wheat flour tortillas
- 2 cups reduced-fat shredded Monterey Jack cheese
- Nonstick cooking spray
- Lime wedges, for serving

To make the guacamole dipping sauce, in a food processor combine the avocados, peas, cilantro, scallion, garlic, jalapeño, lime juice, cumin, and salt. Puree until the mixture is smooth and bright green. Add the yogurt and pulse a few times to lighten up the guacamole and make it creamy. If the guacamole sauce is too thick, add more lime juice or water, a little at a time. Cover with plastic wrap and set aside in the fridge while preparing the quesadillas.

To make the quesadillas, put a skillet over medium-high heat and coat with the oil. When the oil is hot, add the pepper and onion; quickly stir to char the vegetables, taking care not to burn them, 3 to 4 minutes. Transfer to a side plate and return the pan to medium-low heat.

Stir in the water, scraping up the charred pepper and onion bits left in the bottom of the pan. Mix in the tomato paste, cocoa powder, and oregano, stirring until completely dissolved.

Add the beans, stirring well to incorporate. Gently cook for 6 to 8 minutes, stirring and mashing the beans with the back of a wooden spoon to create a thick paste. Add water if needed to keep the beans from sticking and burning. The refried beans should be moist and spreadable, not dry or soupy. You should have about 1 cup.

To assemble, lay 4 tortillas out on a work surface and evenly spread ¼ cup of the refried beans on each to cover. Sprinkle each with ½ cup of cheese and scatter some charred peppers and onions across the top. Cover with the remaining 4 tortillas and press down with your hands.

Put a cast-iron skillet or nonstick griddle over medium-high heat. Spray with nonstick cooking spray. Put the quesadillas in the hot pan and cook until the bottoms of the tortillas are nicely toasted and the cheese begins to melt, about 2 minutes. Keep an eye on them; if the tortillas start to brown too quickly, reduce the heat to medium. Carefully flip the tortillas over with a spatula and gently press down, taking care not to let the cheese ooze out. Cook for another minute, until the undersides are golden and crisp.

Remove the quesadillas from the pan and cut into quarters or eighths. Garnish with lime wedges and serve with guacamole dipping sauce.

Per serving: 286 calories, 12 g total fat (5 g saturated), 15 mg cholesterol, 625 mg sodium, 16 g protein, 15 g fiber, 31 g carb

Garlicky Green Olive Hummus

There are as many varieties of hummus these days as there are people who love this simple, nutritious dip. Here, briny green olives add rich texture and flavor and supply heart-healthy fats. This hummus is protein- and fiber-rich, so you need only a small serving to fill you up. Pair it with fresh vegetables or baked whole wheat pita triangles (see page 31) for an easy appetizer or snack. You can also use this dip as a spread for sandwiches—it makes an excellent, and healthier, stand-in for mayonnaise.

SERVES 8 (MAKES 2 CUPS)

1 (15-ounce) can chickpeas (garbanzo beans), drained and rinsed

½ cup pimento-stuffed green cocktail olives, drained and rinsed (about 10 olives)

¼ cup fresh flat-leaf parsley, coarsely chopped

1 scallion, white and green parts, coarsely chopped

2 garlic cloves, coarsely chopped

Juice of 1 lemon

2 tablespoons extra-virgin olive oil

1 teaspoon ground cumin

Pinch of cayenne pepper

¼ cup low-sodium vegetable broth or water

In a food processor, combine the chickpeas, olives, parsley, scallion, and garlic. Pulse several times, until the mixture is chunky. Add the lemon juice, oil, cumin, and pepper. Pulse a few more times to incorporate. Now puree with the motor running and gradually pour in the broth and puree until combined.

Serve immediately or cover and refrigerate for up to three days.

Per serving (¼ cup): 110 calories, 5 g total fat (>1 g saturated), 0 mg cholesterol, 256 mg sodium, 3 g protein, 3 g fiber, 14 g carb

Quinoa "Fried" Rice, page 61

Part 3

LIGHTENED-UP
CARBS

Grilled Vegetable Lasagna with Mushroom Sauce

Recipe by Chef Laura Vitale

Being Italian, Chef Laura appreciates a good lasagna as much as anyone, so when it came to overhauling this dish, she was serious about keeping its classic flavors intact. To cut down on carbs and calories, she swapped out two of the pasta layers for grilled vegetables, and in place of a meat sauce she created a delicious mushroom sauce. The cheese received a rehab as well, with a mixture of part-skim ricotta, low-fat cottage cheese, Parmesan, and low-fat mozzarella standing in for the heavy cheeses in the original recipe. With a thick tomato sauce and bubbling cheese on top, this healthy lasagna has all the appeal of its classic counterparts, but at less than 300 calories per serving, you can enjoy this version any night of the week!

SERVES 8

SAUCE:

1 tablespoon olive oil

1 small yellow onion, finely chopped

1 small red bell pepper, halved, seeded, and finely diced

10 ounces cremini mushrooms, stemmed, wiped clean, and sliced

¼ teaspoon kosher salt

½ teaspoon freshly ground black pepper

1 teaspoon Italian seasoning

2 garlic cloves, minced

½ cup dry red wine, such as Cabernet Sauvignon

1 (10-ounce) package frozen spinach, thawed, liquid squeezed out

1 (28-ounce) can low-sodium crushed tomatoes

2 tablespoons chopped fresh basil

LASAGNA:

Nonstick cooking spray

1 large zucchini, sliced on the diagonal about ¼-inch thick

1 large eggplant, sliced into ¼-inch rounds

1 cup part-skim ricotta cheese

1 cup low-fat cottage cheese

⅓ cup grated Parmesan cheese

1 large egg

¼ cup chopped fresh flat-leaf parsley

1 teaspoon granulated garlic

1 teaspoon granulated onion

6 no-boil lasagna noodles

½ cup low-fat shredded mozzarella cheese

To prepare the sauce, put a pot over medium heat and coat with the oil. When the oil is hot, add the onion, pepper, and mushrooms. Cook and stir until the vegetables become tender, 7 to 10 minutes. Season with salt, pepper, and Italian seasoning. Add the garlic and cook, stirring, to combine, about 1 minute.

Pour in the wine, stirring, and cook until reduced by half, 2 to 3 minutes. Add the thawed spinach and crushed tomatoes. Reduce the heat to medium-low and gently simmer until the sauce is thickened slightly, about 10 minutes. Add the basil at the end. While the sauce is cooking, prepare the rest of the lasagna.

Coat a grill pan with nonstick spray and put over medium-high heat or preheat an oven broiler. If using the broiler, arrange the eggplant and zucchini in a single layer on two nonstick baking pans. Spray the zucchini and eggplant with nonstick spray. Grill or broil in batches, turning the vegetables once, until they are tender and lightly browned and have released most of their moisture, about 3 to 4 minutes per side. Set the vegetables aside.

In a large bowl, mix together the ricotta, cottage cheese, Parmesan, egg, parsley, and granulated garlic and onion.

Preheat the oven to 375°F. Using a 9-by-13-inch baking dish, ladle enough sauce into the dish to just cover the bottom. Slightly overlap 3 lasagna noodles lengthwise so they completely cover the bottom of the dish, with no gaps. Top the noodles with one-third of the cheese mixture, spreading it evenly with a rubber spatula. Shingle the slices of grilled zucchini in an even layer on top to cover. Spread another layer of the cheese mixture, followed by a ladle of sauce. Repeat the layering process with the eggplant, cheese, and sauce. Finally, top with the 3 remaining lasagna noodles and remaining sauce.

Cover the lasagna with aluminum foil and bake for 30 minutes. Remove the foil, top with the mozzarella, and bake for another 2 minutes, until the cheese has melted. Allow the lasagna to cool for 10 minutes before cutting into squares.

Per serving: 261 calories, 9 g total fat (4 g saturated), 47 mg cholesterol, 384 mg sodium, 18 g protein, 6 g fiber, 28 g carb

Chef Tip: No-Boil Noodles

No-boil, oven-ready lasagna noodles can be layered with other ingredients in a lasagna dish without the hassle of pre-boiling. They're a great, convenient option because they can be used straight from the package, saving time and effort.

Linguine with Clam Sauce

Linguine with clam sauce is an Italian seaside favorite. Typically made with bottled clam juice and knobs of butter, this lightened-up version uses only one tablespoon of butter in the entire dish. Steaming the clams in white wine and water allows them to release their own natural briny liquid, so there's no need for the bottled stuff, which helps keep the sodium content of this dish in check. Clams are a good source of protein and make a great alternative to the same old seafood choices. Flecked with parsley and infused with the bright flavor of fresh lemon, this simple and elegant pasta dish feels like summer at the beach.

SERVES 4

¾ pound linguine

½ cup dry white wine

¼ cup water

Juice of 1 lemon

1 shallot, minced

3 garlic cloves, thinly sliced

2 bay leaves

¼ teaspoon red pepper flakes

1 dozen littleneck clams, rinsed and scrubbed

½ cup chopped fresh flat-leaf parsley, plus more for garnish

1 tablespoon unsalted butter

Bring a large pot of water to a boil over high heat. Add the linguine and stir well. Cook, stirring occasionally, until al dente ("with a bite"), about 8 minutes.

Put a wide, shallow skillet (with a lid) over medium heat. Pour in the wine, water, and lemon juice; add the shallot, garlic, bay leaves, and pepper flakes. Stir to combine and bring to a simmer. As soon as you see steam coming from the liquid, add the clams and cover the pan. Steam the clams for 6 to 7 minutes, shaking the pan from time to time, until all or most of the clams open. Discard any clams that do not open.

Drain the pasta in a colander set in the sink, and then add to the clams, along with the parsley and butter. Toss with tongs for 1 minute, until well coated.

Serve the linguine and clam sauce in shallow pasta bowls, arranging the open clams on top. Garnish with chopped parsley.

Per serving: 396 calories, 5 g total fat (2 g saturated), 16 mg cholesterol, 173 mg sodium, 16 g protein, 3 g fiber, 68 g carb

Creamy Butternut Squash Shells and Cheese

Recipe by Chef Candice Kumai

When Chef Candice was given the challenge of rehabbing a family's favorite mac-and-cheese recipe, she swapped out the heavy cheese sauce for a homemade butternut squash puree, which has a similar color and a delicious, rich flavor. While there is no butter or oil in this recipe—and just a little bit of cheese—it still tastes rich and creamy. All told, Chef Candice's rehab saved more than 500 calories and 40 grams of fat! Baking this mac and cheese in individual ramekins makes for a sophisticated presentation and keeps portions under control.

SERVES 8

SQUASH PUREE:

Nonstick cooking spray

1 (2-pound) butternut squash, peeled, halved, seeded, cubed (about 4 cups)

2 cups unsweetened plain almond milk

2 cups low-sodium chicken or vegetable broth

6 garlic cloves, smashed

2 sprigs fresh thyme

1 teaspoon kosher salt

1 (1-pound) box mini-shells

TOPPING:

¾ cup panko (Japanese-style bread crumbs)

1 tablespoon chopped fresh flat-leaf parsley

½ teaspoon coarse salt

2 garlic cloves, minced

½ teaspoon red pepper flakes (optional)

¾ cup finely shredded Gruyère or Swiss cheese

Preheat the oven to 375°F. Coat 8 (6-ounce) ramekins/soufflé cups with nonstick spray. Set aside.

Place a large pot over medium heat. Add the squash, almond milk, broth, garlic, thyme, and salt. Simmer until the squash is fork tender, about 20 minutes. Remove the thyme sprigs from the squash mixture. Transfer the squash, including the liquid, to a food processor or blender. Puree until the mixture is velvety smooth.

Meanwhile, cook the shells in boiling water until al dente. Drain and rinse with cool water. Put the shells in a mixing bowl and pour in the squash puree. Mix to combine. Spoon the pasta mixture into the prepared ramekins; you should have about 6 cups. Set the ramekins on a baking pan.

To prepare the topping: In a large mixing bowl, combine the bread crumbs, parsley, salt, garlic, and red pepper flakes, if using. Sprinkle 2 tablespoons of the crumb topping evenly over each ramekin. Cover the tops of the ramekins with aluminum foil, tucking it under the edges of the baking pan. Bake until golden and bubbling, about 20 minutes.

Remove the foil from the baking pan. Sprinkle the cheese evenly over the top of each ramekin and bake for an additional 5 minutes, uncovered.

Per serving: 343 calories, 5 g total fat (2 g saturated), 11 mg cholesterol, 477 mg sodium, 14 g protein, 4 g fiber, 61 g carb

Makeover Mac and Cheese

Recipe by Chef Govind Armstrong

As a father, Chef Govind is used to cooking for mac-and-cheese fanatics, so this rehab has been tested out in his home kitchen more than once. He swapped out butter and cream for reduced-fat dairy products and added a dose of veggies by whipping up a velvety-smooth puree of steamed cauliflower. Not only does the cauliflower add a nutritional boost, but it makes the sauce extra creamy. If you have a picky eater or vegetable hater at home, this recipe is a great way to sneak some veggies into dinner!

SERVES 8

Nonstick cooking spray

2 cups coarsely chopped cauliflower florets

1 medium onion, coarsely chopped

2 garlic cloves

½ cup plain nonfat Greek-style yogurt

2 tablespoons nondairy butter spread, such as Earth Balance

2 tablespoons whole wheat flour

2 cups low-fat milk, plus ¼ cup if needed

1 tablespoon Dijon mustard

1 cup small-curd fat-free cottage cheese

2 cups shredded low-fat cheddar cheese, preferably white

1 cup shredded low-fat mozzarella cheese, preferably smoked

1½ pounds whole grain elbow macaroni, cooked al dente

TOPPING:

½ cup coarsely ground Ritz crackers (about 6 crackers)

½ teaspoon paprika

1 tablespoon finely chopped fresh flat-leaf parsley

¼ teaspoon granulated garlic

1 tablespoon olive oil

Preheat the oven to 325°F. Coat a 13-by-9-inch baking dish with nonstick spray. Set aside.

Place a steamer basket in the bottom of a 3-quart pot. Add enough water to just touch the bottom of the basket. Bring the water to a boil over high heat. Arrange the cauliflower, onion, and garlic evenly around the perforated basket. Reduce the heat to medium. Cover the pot with a lid and steam the vegetables for 15 minutes, or until the cauliflower is fork tender. Carefully remove the basket and transfer the vegetables to a food processor. Add the yogurt and puree until the vegetables are completely smooth. Set aside at room temperature.

In a large pot or deep skillet over low heat, melt the butter substitute and sprinkle in the flour. Stir constantly with a wooden spoon or whisk to cook out the taste of the flour and create a thick paste; take care not to allow the flour to brown.

Add the milk and the Dijon and whisk until smooth. Mix in the cottage cheese, cheddar, and mozzarella. Continue to stir to fully incorporate, until cheese is melted.

Add the cooked macaroni and the reserved cauliflower puree. Gently fold the pasta into the sauce to thoroughly coat, adding ¼ cup of milk if the mixture gets too thick.

Pour the cheesy macaroni mixture into the prepared casserole dish, spreading it out evenly. Bake for 30 minutes, until bubbly. In the meantime, prepare the topping.

To prepare the topping, in a small bowl combine the cracker crumbs, paprika, parsley, granulated garlic, and olive oil. Mix until the ingredients are well distributed.

Spread the topping evenly over the macaroni and cheese. Return the casserole dish to the oven for 8 to 10 minutes, until the topping is golden brown. Allow the mac and cheese to rest for 5 minutes before serving.

Per serving: 506 calories, 12 g total fat (5 g saturated), 19 mg cholesterol, 523 mg sodium, 31 g protein, 8 g fiber, 75 g carb

REHAB TIP: CAULIFLOWER Puréed cauliflower makes a delicious and healthy stand-in for starchy vegetables like potatoes, and also adds creaminess to soups and sauces for very few calories. Try steaming fresh or frozen cauliflower and then mashing or puréeing it with a little bit of light butter for a nutritious and low-carb version of mashed potatoes.

Barley Risotto with Fennel and Radicchio

Traditional risotto is made with arborio rice, which provides that distinctive velvety texture that makes risotto so luxurious, but it's not exactly the healthiest choice. Believe it or not, barley is an excellent stand-in for arborio rice—pearl barley adds a nutty, supple creaminess to the risotto and is an excellent source of fiber. The addition of fennel, garlic, and radicchio adds earthiness and peppery notes to this one-pot wonder. This dish tastes so rich and refined, no one will believe that it doesn't contain an ounce of butter or cream.

SERVES 6

4 cups low-sodium vegetable broth

4 cups water

2 tablespoons olive oil

1 small onion, minced

1 fennel bulb, quartered, cored, and cut into thin strips, fronds reserved

2 garlic cloves, minced

3 sprigs fresh thyme

1 cup dry white wine, such as Pinot Grigio

1½ cups pearl barley, rinsed and drained

¼ teaspoon kosher salt

½ teaspoon freshly ground black pepper

1 small head radicchio, quartered, cored, and cut crosswise into thin slivers

¾ cup freshly grated Parmesan cheese (about 1½ ounces)

Chopped fresh flat-leaf parsley, for garnish

Pour the broth and water into a pot and bring to a simmer over low heat.

Put a wide, shallow skillet over medium heat and coat with 1 tablespoon of the oil. When the oil is hot, add the onion, fennel, garlic, and thyme. Cook, stirring, until the vegetables begin to soften but not brown, about 2 minutes. Pour in the wine and cook until the onion and fennel are tender, about 3 minutes.

Add the barley. Cook, stirring often, until the barley is lightly toasted and opaque and the grains begin to crackle. Season with salt and pepper. Begin adding the simmering broth, a couple of ladlefuls (about 1 cup) at a time. The broth should just cover the barley. Stir with a wooden spoon until the barley has absorbed all the liquid, then add another cup. You may not need all of the broth. Cook, stirring often, until the broth is almost completely absorbed.

Cook until the barley is tender but still chewy, 45 to 50 minutes. Fold in the radicchio and Parmesan and cook another minute or two. Remove the thyme sprigs, drizzle with the remaining tablespoon of olive oil, and remove from the heat.

Garnish with chopped parsley. Serve immediately.

Chef Tip: Barley

Barley is a high-fiber, low-fat grain with a nutty flavor and texture. The most common types of barley are hulled and pearl (or pearled). Hulled barley can be difficult to find in supermarkets and must be soaked for a long time before cooking. Pearl barley, however, is widely available and cooks much more quickly. Try it instead of brown rice in your favorite recipes.

Per serving: 324 calories, 8 g total fat (2.5 g saturated), 9 mg cholesterol, 357 mg sodium, 10 g protein, 10 g fiber, 47 g carb

Scalloped Potatoes Au Gratin

Recipe by Chef Calvin Harris

Scalloped potatoes are a staple dish at many family get-togethers. Who can forget their grandmother's famous potato casserole? When Chef Calvin took on the challenge of rehabbing a dish made with heavy cream, butter, and a mountain of cheese, he eliminated the butter entirely and instead cooked the potatoes in fat-free half-and-half. The starch in the potatoes thickens the sauce naturally. He also reduced the amount of cheese but selected strongly flavored cheeses such as aged cheddar and smoked Gouda. This rich potato dish is just as creamy and delicious as you remember it—but has about half the calories.

SERVES 6

Nonstick cooking spray

1 pint fat-free half-and-half

2 garlic cloves, minced

½ teaspoon ground nutmeg

2 pounds russet potatoes, peeled and thinly sliced (preferably on a mandolin)

1 teaspoon coarse salt

½ teaspoon freshly ground black pepper

½ cup shredded aged sharp cheddar cheese

½ cup shredded smoked Gouda cheese

½ cup panko (Japanese-style bread crumbs)

3 green onions, white and greens parts, chopped

Preheat the oven to 400°F. Coat a 2-quart baking dish with nonstick cooking spray. Set aside.

Place a Dutch oven or pot over medium heat. Add the fat-free half-and-half, garlic, and nutmeg. Gently simmer for 3 to 5 minutes, stirring occasionally. Add the potatoes to the pot, gently stirring the potatoes into the base mixture to coat. Season with salt and pepper. Allow the starch of the potato to thicken the sauce. Add ¼ cup of each type of cheese and continue to cook, gently stirring the mixture until the potatoes begin to get tender.

Pour the potato mixture into the prepared baking dish, spreading it out evenly. Top with the remaining cheese and the bread crumbs. Spray a thin layer of nonstick cooking spray all over the surface.

Bake for 45 minutes or until the potatoes are tender and golden brown on top. Let stand for 5 minutes before serving and sprinkle with chopped green onions.

 To watch a how-to video for this recipe, check out www.RecipeRehab.com.

Per serving: 251 calories, 6 g total fat (4 g saturated), 21 mg cholesterol, 541 mg sodium, 9 g protein, 2 g fiber, 37 g carb

> **REHAB TIP: HALF AND HALF** Regular cream contains saturated fat, and eating too many foods high in saturated fat can lead to high blood cholesterol. Fat-free half-and-half is made mostly of skim milk instead of half cream and half whole milk, so it helps you cut back on saturated fat but looks and tastes like traditional half-and-half. It's a great swap for people who want to enjoy thick, creamy sauces but want to lower their fat and calorie intake.

Spaghetti and Turkey Meatballs

Recipe by Chef Laura Vitale

When Chef Laura went head-to-head against Chef Aida in the Spaghetti and Meatball Challenge, they were faced with a family recipe that came in at 1,500 calories and nine servings of refined carbohydrates on just one plate. Chef Laura reduced the fat and calories and increased the fiber content by substituting lean ground turkey for beef, swapping whole wheat pasta for white, and reducing the portion size of the pasta. Chef Laura's tip for making perfectly sized meatballs? "Use a small ice cream scoop. It not only keeps your hands clean but also keeps portions in check."

SERVES 6

MEATBALLS:

Nonstick cooking spray

1¼ pounds lean ground turkey, such as Jennie-O® Lean Ground Turkey

2 tablespoons store-bought pesto

2 garlic cloves, minced

2 slices white bread, coarsely chopped and pulsed in a food processor

¼ cup freshly grated Parmesan cheese

1 large egg white

¼ teaspoon kosher salt

¼ teaspoon freshly ground black pepper

SAUCE:

1 tablespoon olive oil

1 small onion, diced

2 garlic cloves, minced

½ cup dry white wine, such as Pinot Grigio

1 (28-ounce) can crushed organic tomatoes

1 (15-ounce) can tomato puree

1 teaspoon dried oregano

¼ teaspoon kosher salt

¼ teaspoon freshly ground black pepper

4 fresh basil leaves, chopped

FOR SERVING:

¾ pound whole wheat spaghetti, cooked al dente

4 fresh basil leaves, chopped

6 tablespoons freshly grated Parmesan cheese

Preheat the oven to 450°F. Line a baking pan with parchment paper and spray with nonstick spray. Set aside.

In a mixing bowl, combine the ground turkey, pesto, garlic, fresh bread crumbs, Parmesan, egg white, salt, and pepper. Mix everything until the meat mixture is well combined. Use a small ice cream scoop to form into 24 equal-size meatballs. Arrange the meatballs side by side on the prepared baking pan. Spray the tops of the meatballs with a little nonstick spray. Refrigerate the meatballs for about 10 minutes, or until firm. Remove the meatballs from the refrigerator and bake for 10 minutes, or until meatballs are no longer pink in the center and juices run clear when a meatball is pierced with a fork.

To prepare the sauce, place a large, deep skillet over medium heat and coat with the oil. When the oil is hot, add the onion and garlic. Cook and stir until the onion begins to soften and brown, about 5 minutes. Pour in the wine and continue to cook until it is almost completely evaporated, about 1 minute.

Add the crushed tomatoes, tomato puree, oregano, salt, and pepper. Stir the ingredients together and simmer for 20 minutes, stirring occasionally.

Remove the baked meatballs from the oven and carefully transfer them into the tomato sauce. Add the fresh basil and simmer for 5 minutes.

To serve, toss the cooked spaghetti with half of the tomato sauce. Divide the spaghetti among six pasta bowls. Top with four meatballs and 1 tablespoon of freshly grated Parmesan cheese. Serve the remaining sauce on the side.

 To watch a how-to video for this recipe, check out www.RecipeRehab.com.

Per serving: 561 calories, 17 g total fat (6 g saturated), 111 mg cholesterol, 589 mg sodium, 38 g protein, 12 g fiber, 63 g carb

Chef Tip: Fresh Bread Crumbs

Using fresh bread crumbs in recipes for meatballs or meatloaf adds moisture and binds the meat together without having to use whole eggs. To make your own bread crumbs, tear several slices of fresh white, French, or whole wheat bread into 1-inch pieces. Place in a food processor or blender; cover and push the pulse button several times to make coarse crumbs. One slice of bread yields about ½ cup crumbs.

Tuscan Tuna and White Bean Casserole

Think of this recipe as a grown-up, modern version of that tuna noodle casserole your mom used to make when you were a kid. It's still a snap to throw together and utilizes pantry staples like canned tuna and white beans (a classic Italian pairing), combined with bread crumbs and dried pasta—but this version has been significantly lightened up and elevated just a little for an adult palate. For an even quicker rendition, simply toss the tuna and white bean sauce with the pasta and skip the baking. Serve with a spinach salad for a balanced, easy weeknight meal.

SERVES 6

Nonstick cooking spray

1 tablespoon canola oil

1 tablespoon light butter, such as Land O'Lakes

1 onion, chopped

3 garlic cloves, minced

¼ teaspoon salt

½ teaspoon freshly ground black pepper

¼ teaspoon red pepper flakes

1 tablespoon fresh rosemary leaves, finely chopped

2 teaspoons Dijon mustard

Juice of ½ lemon

1 (15-ounce) can white cannellini beans, drained and rinsed

2 (5-ounce) cans no-salt-added chunk light tuna packed in water, drained

1 pint cherry tomatoes, halved

1 cup low-sodium vegetable broth

6 ounces spinach linguine, broken in half, cooked al dente

¼ cup plain bread crumbs

1 teaspoon Italian seasoning

Preheat the oven to 375°F. Coat a 13-by-9-inch baking dish with nonstick spray. Set aside.

Put a large skillet over medium heat and add the oil and butter. When the butter is foamy, add the onion and garlic. Cook and stir for 2 to 3 minutes, until soft; season with salt, pepper, and red pepper flakes. Sprinkle in the rosemary, then stir in the mustard and lemon juice. Fold in the beans and tuna. Cook and stir for 1 minute to incorporate. Add the tomatoes and continue to cook for 3 minutes, until they break down and soften.

Add the broth to the skillet and simmer until the mixture thickens slightly, about 5 minutes. Remove the tuna-and-bean mixture from the heat.

Put the linguine in a large bowl and pour the tuna mixture over the noodles. Toss to combine. Transfer the noodle mixture to the prepared baking dish. In a small bowl, combine the bread crumbs and Italian seasoning. Sprinkle the seasoned bread crumbs evenly on top. Bake, uncovered, for 10 minutes, until the top is golden and the filling is bubbly.

Per serving: 295 calories, 6 g total fat (1 g saturated), 21 mg cholesterol, 354 mg sodium, 21 g protein, 6 g fiber, 41 g carb

Thai Noodles with Peanut-Ginger Sauce

A staple in Thai cuisine, peanut sauce is typically high in fat and sugar. Thinning the peanut butter with hot water reduces the fat and calories while keeping that nutty, rich flavor. Spiked with lime, ginger, and garlic, this sauce delivers all of the notes you'd expect from a Thai noodle dish. If you're a fan of pad Thai but have been avoiding it because of the calories, this is your new go-to recipe.

SERVES 4

½ pound dried flat rice noodles/sticks

SAUCE:

6 tablespoons creamy peanut butter

½ cup hot water

3 tablespoons reduced-sodium soy sauce

3 tablespoons unseasoned rice vinegar

Juice of 2 limes

1 tablespoon peeled and grated fresh ginger

2 garlic cloves, minced

2 teaspoons Sriracha hot sauce

1 teaspoon dark brown sugar

NOODLES:

2 teaspoons canola oil

1 bunch asparagus, chopped (about ½ cup)

½ cup shredded carrot

½ small red bell pepper, cored and thinly sliced

2 scallions, white and green parts, chopped

1 cup bean sprouts

¼ cup fresh mint leaves, coarsely chopped

¼ cup fresh basil leaves, preferably Thai, coarsely chopped

2 tablespoons chopped unsalted peanuts

Put the noodles in a bowl and cover with boiling water. Soak until the noodles are pliable, 3 to 8 minutes. (Later cooking in the pan will soften them even more.) Drain the noodles and set aside while preparing the other ingredients.

To make the sauce, in a blender combine the peanut butter, hot water, soy sauce, vinegar, lime juice, ginger, garlic, hot sauce, and sugar. Blend on high until the peanut butter has thinned out and the ingredients are well incorporated.

Put a large skillet or wok over medium-high heat and coat with the oil. When the oil is hot, add the asparagus, carrot, pepper, and scallions. Cook and stir until the vegetables release their moisture and begin to brown, about 5 minutes. Add the drained noodles to the pan. Using two utensils and a lifting-tossing motion to separate the strands, stir-fry the noodles for 1 minute. If the rice noodles are still too firm, drizzle with 1 to 2 tablespoons of water to help them cook. When the noodles are well incorporated, remove from the heat and toss to evenly distribute.

Scrape the noodle-vegetable mixture into a serving bowl. Pour in the peanut sauce, tossing well to coat the noodles and keep from sticking. Add the bean sprouts, mint, and basil, tossing well to incorporate. Divide the Thai noodles and vegetables among four plates and garnish with chopped peanuts.

Per serving: 432 calories, 17 g total fat (3 g saturated), 0 mg cholesterol, 572 mg sodium, 10 g protein, 24 g fiber, 64 g carb

Spaghetti Squash and Quinoa "Meatballs"

Recipe by Chef Aida Mollenkamp

Chef Aida's take on spaghetti and meatballs is unlike any other you're likely to find out there—it's not made with pasta *or* meat! This vegetarian dish is made with spaghetti squash, which is lower in carbs and calories than pasta, and quinoa "meatballs" made from grains and mushrooms. You can make each of the components of this dish ahead of time and keep them refrigerated until you're ready to assemble the entire dish. Be careful when cutting into the squash—Chef Aida advises piercing the skin of the squash with a knife a few times and cooking it in the microwave for 1 minute to soften it before cutting.

SERVES 6

SQUASH:

2 spaghetti squash (about 5 pounds total), halved lengthwise and seeded

2 teaspoons olive oil

¼ teaspoon kosher salt

¼ teaspoon freshly ground black pepper

MEATBALLS:

¾ cup quinoa, rinsed

2 teaspoons olive oil

1 onion, finely chopped

1 garlic clove, minced

1 tablespoon finely chopped fresh thyme leaves

¼ teaspoon kosher salt

½ teaspoon freshly ground black pepper

12 ounces cremini mushrooms, stemmed, wiped clean, and finely chopped

2 tablespoons tomato paste

2 large eggs, lightly beaten

½ cup whole wheat panko (Japanese-style bread crumbs)

¼ cup freshly grated Parmesan cheese

⅓ cup finely chopped fresh flat-leaf parsley

Nonstick cooking spray

SAUCE:

2 teaspoons olive oil

1 onion, finely chopped

¼ teaspoon freshly ground black pepper

¼ cup dry red wine, such as Cabernet Sauvignon

1 (28-ounce) can low-sodium crushed tomatoes

2 teaspoons unrefined cane sugar

To make the squash, preheat the oven to 375°F.

Drizzle the flesh of the squash with oil and season with salt and pepper. Place it, cut side down, on a baking pan and roast until fork-tender, about 45 minutes.

Scrape the squash with a fork to remove the flesh in long strands. Put in a large mixing bowl and cover to keep warm. Keep the oven on for the meatballs.

To make the quinoa for the meatballs, in a pot combine the quinoa with 1½ cups of water over medium-high heat. When the water comes to a boil, cover, reduce heat to low, and simmer until the water is absorbed and the quinoa fluffs up, about 15 minutes. The quinoa is good to go when you can see the curlicue popping out of each grain. The water should be absorbed; if it's not, drain any excess. Remove the quinoa from the heat and fluff with a fork. Transfer the quinoa to a mixing bowl.

Put a large skillet over medium heat and coat with the oil. When the oil is hot, add the onion and cook until soft. Stir in the garlic, thyme, salt, and pepper. Cook until fragrant, about 30 seconds.

Stir in the mushrooms and continue to cook until lightly browned, about 10 minutes. Stir in the tomato paste and cook until incorporated, about 1 minute. Remove from the heat and scrape into the quinoa. Set aside to cool, at least 10 minutes.

When the vegetable mixture is cool, add the eggs, bread crumbs, cheese, and parsley and mix thoroughly. Coat a baking pan with nonstick cooking spray. Dampen hands with water and then measure out heaping 1-tablespoon portions and roll the mixture into 30 to 32 (1-inch) meatballs, placing on the baking pan as you go along.

Bake at 375°F until warmed through, about 15 to 20 minutes. (Meatballs can be made up to 2 days in advance.)

To make the sauce, put a pot over medium heat and coat with the oil. When the oil is hot, add the onion and season with pepper. Cook and stir for 3 minutes, until softened. Pour in the wine and stir until almost completely evaporated, about 1 minute. Pour in the crushed tomatoes and sprinkle in the sugar, stirring to incorporate. Simmer for 15 minutes, stirring occasionally.

To serve, divide the spaghetti squash among six plates and top with five to six meatballs per serving and a few ladles of sauce.

Per serving: 358 calories, 10 g total fat (2 g saturated), 65 mg cholesterol, 351 mg sodium, 14 g protein, 10 g fiber, 55 g carb

Cajun Shrimp and Grits

The amount of fat and sodium found in a typical bowl of shrimp and grits can make this Southern favorite a nutritional nightmare. But grits, which are made from ground dried corn kernels, are on their own quite healthy, providing necessary complex carbohydrates for energy. It's only when you cook them in butter, lard, or cream that you get into trouble! Here, low-sodium chicken broth, with just a small amount of low-fat milk, lends enough creaminess that you won't miss all that fat. Infused with smoky Cajun spices, the shrimp stand up perfectly to the pool of grits, creating a flavorful but healthy rendition of this time-honored dish.

SERVES 4

GRITS:

2 cups low-sodium chicken broth

½ cup yellow cornmeal

¼ cup low-fat milk

1 tablespoon unsalted butter

¼ teaspoon kosher salt

¼ teaspoon freshly ground black pepper

SHRIMP:

1 pound medium peeled and deveined shrimp, tails on (about 20)

2 tablespoons salt-free Cajun seasoning (such as Frontier)

1 tablespoon canola oil

1 small onion, chopped

2 scallions, white and green parts, chopped

½ red bell pepper, cored and thinly sliced

3 garlic cloves, minced

1 bay leaf

2 tablespoons all-purpose flour

1½ cups low-sodium chicken broth

Juice of ½ lemon

2 tablespoons chopped fresh flat-leaf parsley, for garnish

Hot sauce, for serving (optional)

To make the grits, place a pot over medium-high heat. Pour in the broth and bring to a boil. Slowly whisk in the cornmeal. When the grits begin to bubble, turn the heat down to medium-low and simmer, stirring frequently with a wooden spoon. Allow to cook for 15 to 20 minutes, until the mixture is smooth and thick. Remove from heat and stir in the low-fat milk and butter. Season with salt and pepper. Cover and keep warm.

To make the shrimp, toss the shrimp with the Cajun seasoning to coat. Put a large skillet over medium heat and coat with the oil. When the oil is hot, add the onion, scallions, bell pepper, garlic, and bay leaf. Cook and stir until the vegetables are tender, 5 to 6 minutes. Sprinkle the flour over the vegetables and stir with a wooden spoon until dissolved.

Once the flour is fully incorporated, slowly pour in the broth and continue to stir to avoid lumps. When the liquid comes to a simmer, add the shrimp. Poach the shrimp for 2 to 3 minutes, until they are firm and pink and the gravy is smooth and thick. Remove from the heat and stir in the lemon juice.

Spoon the grits onto each plate and top with the shrimp mixture. Garnish with chopped parsley and serve with hot sauce, if desired.

Per serving: 215 calories, 9 g total fat (3 g saturated), 46 mg cholesterol, 365 mg sodium, 11 g protein, 2 g fiber, 26 g carb

Quinoa "Fried" Rice

Recipe by Chef Govind Armstrong

Fried rice . . . the name says it all. Chef Govind rehabbed this high-cal takeout dish by swapping white rice for a mix of quinoa and brown rice and adding in lots of colorful vegetables like collard greens, pea sprouts, and carrots. But don't let these suggestions stop you—this recipe is really just a healthy base, so you should feel free to get creative. Add as many vegetables as you like—snow peas, green beans, or broccoli would all work well. You could also add a lean protein like shrimp, tofu, or chicken. This recipe is an easy and delicious way to use up leftover brown rice from another meal, and it comes together in just 30 minutes.

SERVES 4

½ cup quinoa, rinsed

1 cup water

Pinch of salt

2 cups cooked brown rice

2 tablespoons canola oil

1 large yellow onion, diced

2 cups chopped collard greens

1 cup frozen peas and carrots, run under cool water for 2 minutes to thaw

½ cup chopped pea sprouts (optional)

3 tablespoons light soy sauce

1 teaspoon sesame oil

Salt and pepper, to taste

Hot sauce (optional)

In a small pot, combine the quinoa, water, and salt; bring to a boil over high heat. Cover, reduce the heat to low, and simmer until the water is absorbed, about 15 minutes. The quinoa is cooked when you can see the curlicue popping out of each grain. Drain any excess water. Remove quinoa from heat and fluff with a fork.

Microwave the brown rice on high for 2 minutes.

Coat a wok or large skillet with the oil and place over medium-high heat. Give the oil a minute to heat up, then add the onion and collard greens; stir-fry for 3 minutes, until vegetables are wilted slightly but still have texture. Add the peas and carrots, sprouts (if using), prepared quinoa, and precooked brown rice. Cook and toss well for 3 to 4 minutes to distribute the ingredients. Moisten with the soy sauce and sesame oil. Toss the ingredients together to heat through; season with salt and pepper.

Spoon the quinoa-and-brown-rice mixture out onto a serving platter. Serve with hot sauce, if desired.

Per serving: 328 calories, 10 g total fat (1 g saturated), 57 mg cholesterol, 423 mg sodium, 9 g protein, 6 g fiber, 51 g carb

Penne Pasta with Roasted Garlic and Arugula Pesto

Pesto, with its combination of pine nuts, fresh basil, garlic, and Parmesan cheese, is a delicious and versatile sauce that's well worth making at home instead of buying jarred. Toss it with pasta, brush it on grilled chicken, or swirl it into healthy dips—you can find a million uses for fresh pesto. This version uses arugula in place of basil, which adds a slightly bitter, peppery flavor. Heart-healthy walnuts take the place of pine nuts, and their crunchy texture makes this pesto really stand out. Here the pesto is paired with whole wheat pasta and a little chopped tomato for an easy and nutritious weeknight meal. (If you're not making pasta, you can use regular water in place of pasta water in the pesto recipe.) The pesto can be refrigerated in an airtight container for up to 4 days, or frozen for up to 3 months.

SERVES 6 (MAKES 1 CUP PESTO)

5 garlic cloves, unpeeled

½ pound whole wheat penne or bow-tie pasta

¼ cup unsalted walnuts, toasted

3 cups arugula leaves, coarsely chopped

½ cup fresh flat-leaf parsley, coarsely chopped

3 tablespoons water or dry white wine

Juice of 1 lemon

3 tablespoons extra-virgin olive oil

1 teaspoon kosher salt

¼ teaspoon red pepper flakes

½ cup grated Pecorino or Parmesan cheese

1 plum (Roma) tomato, finely chopped

Put the garlic in a dry skillet over medium heat and roast, shaking the pan occasionally, until the skins are brown in spots, about 6 minutes. When the garlic is cool enough to handle, peel off the charred skins.

Bring a large pot of water to a boil over high heat. Add the pasta and stir well. Cook, stirring occasionally, until al dente, tender but not mushy, about 10 minutes. Try to time it so that the pesto is done when the pasta is ready. You'll need to reserve ¼ cup of the pasta water to moisten the pesto at the end.

For the pesto, using a food processor, add the walnuts and pulse a few times to chop them up. Add a couple of handfuls of arugula and pulse until chopped enough that you have room to add the remaining ingredients. Add the rest of the arugula, parsley, water or white wine, lemon juice, and oil. Process until combined. Add the pan-roasted garlic, salt, red pepper flakes, and cheese and use the pulse button to incorporate all ingredients.

Drain the pasta in a colander set in the sink. Add the reserved pasta water a little at a time to the pesto. Puree until the pesto takes on a looser consistency.

To serve, put the hot pasta in a serving bowl and add the pesto. Toss well to cover evenly. Garnish with chopped tomato.

Per serving: 277 calories, 14 g total fat (3 g saturated), 7 mg cholesterol, 454 mg sodium, 8 g protein, 4 g fiber, 32 g carb

Carnitas Tacos with Roasted Tomatillos, page 70

Part 4

DINNER
TONIGHT

Barbecue Chicken Pizza

Recipe by Chef Calvin Harris

When Chef Calvin was tasked with making over a family's favorite recipe for barbecue chicken pizza, the first simple change he made was to toss the high-sodium, high-sugar bottled barbecue sauce and make his own version from scratch. Using a pungent blend of spices mixed with salt-free ketchup, he was able to re-create the smoky-sweet flavor of the family's favorite bottled sauce in a much healthier way. Chef Calvin also replaced the family's beloved rotisserie chicken with skinless chicken breasts and went much easier on the cheese. In all, he shaved off almost 400 calories per serving without skimping one bit on flavor.

SERVES 6

BARBECUE SAUCE:

½ sweet onion, grated with a box grater

1 garlic clove, minced

½ cup no-salt-added ketchup

½ cup low-sodium chicken broth

2 tablespoons apple cider vinegar

1 tablespoon molasses

2 teaspoons Dijon mustard

2 teaspoons Worcestershire sauce

1 teaspoon hot sauce, such as Tabasco

½ teaspoon paprika

½ teaspoon ground cumin

PIZZA:

Nonstick cooking spray

1 (12-inch) thin whole wheat pizza crust, such as Boboli

2 teaspoons olive oil

2 garlic cloves, minced

1 pound skinless, boneless, chicken breast, raw and chopped

½ teaspoon ground cumin

½ teaspoon chipotle chile powder

½ teaspoon freshly ground black pepper

¾ cup shredded reduced-fat mozzarella cheese

¼ cup shredded smoked Gouda cheese

4 scallions, white and green parts, chopped

½ small red onion, thinly sliced

½ red bell pepper, seeded and thinly sliced

½ poblano pepper, seeded and thinly sliced

⅓ cup frozen corn, thawed

2 tablespoons chopped fresh cilantro

To make the barbecue sauce, combine the onion, garlic, ketchup, broth, vinegar, molasses, mustard, Worcestershire, hot sauce, paprika, and cumin in a small pot. Bring to a simmer over medium heat. Reduce the heat to low and simmer, stirring frequently, until slightly thickened, 10 to 15 minutes. Remove from heat, cover, and set aside.

To make the pizza, preheat the oven to 400°F. Coat a baking pan with nonstick cooking spray and put the pizza crust in the pan. Set aside.

Place a skillet over medium heat and coat with the oil. When the oil is hot, add the garlic, chicken, cumin, chipotle powder, and pepper. Sauté until golden brown, 7 to 10 minutes.

Spread the barbecue sauce over the pizza crust. Sprinkle both cheeses evenly around, then add the chicken mixture, scallion, red onion, bell pepper, poblano, corn, and cilantro. Bake for 12 to 15 minutes, until golden brown.

Cut into 6 slices with a pizza cutter and serve immediately.

Per serving (one slice): 330 calories, 9 g total fat (2.5 g saturated), 45 mg cholesterol, 471 mg sodium, 24 g protein, 6 g fiber, 42 g carb

Chef Tip: Pizza

Homemade pizza is a great alternative to takeout, and the whole family can get involved in the kitchen. When you use a store-bought crust, it becomes a quick, easy weeknight meal. Pizzas provide a great opportunity for getting your kids to eat vegetables—pile them high with peppers, onions, tomatoes, or any other vegetables, and use just a little cheese.

Mexican Tlayuda (Pizza)

Recipe by Chef Aida Mollenkamp

Tlayuda is a traditional street food in Mexico. It's made by charring a handmade tortilla and smothering it with refried black beans, piling it with a heap of cabbage, and topping with an assortment of garnishes. This version swaps the tortilla for pizza dough, refried beans for black beans, and adds reduced-fat cheese and fresh veggies.

SERVES 6

2 tablespoons olive oil

12 ounces 98% lean ground chicken

1 teaspoon ground cumin

4 garlic cloves, minced

1 cup sweet corn kernels, either fresh or frozen and thawed

1 large red bell pepper, halved, cored, and diced

3 scallions, white and green parts, thinly sliced

12 (6-inch) whole wheat tortillas

2 (15-ounce) cans black beans, drained and rinsed

½ cup part-skim shredded mozzarella cheese

FOR GARNISH (OPTIONAL):

1 handful fresh cilantro leaves

Salsa verde (tomatillo salsa)

1 ripe medium avocado, halved, pitted, and sliced

Nonfat plain Greek yogurt

Preheat the oven to 400°F.

Coat a large nonstick skillet with 1 tablespoon of oil and place over medium-high heat. When the oil is hot, add the chicken and cumin. Break up chicken with a wooden spoon and cook for about 5 to 10 minutes, until chicken is no longer pink.

Remove the chicken to a side plate with a slotted spoon, reserve any drippings, and return the skillet to medium-high heat. Add the garlic and corn and cook, stirring frequently, until kernels are golden brown. Stir in bell pepper and cook for another 5 minutes. Remove vegetables from the heat and stir in the reserved chicken and the scallions.

Drain and rinse black beans. Remove excess moisture, then place in a medium-size bowl. Mash beans until they resemble the consistency of refried beans.

Brush both sides of the tortillas with the remaining oil. Arrange the tortillas on two baking pans. Bake until golden, about 5 minutes. Divide the beans, cheese, and the chicken-and-vegetable mixture evenly among the tortillas. Bake until the cheese is bubbly, and the tortillas are crisp on the edges, another 5 to 10 minutes. Top with desired garnishes and serve.

Per serving (2 tortillas): 403 calories, 12 g total fat (4 g saturated), 52 mg cholesterol, 865 mg sodium, 31 g protein, 28 g fiber, 54 g carb

Chef Tip: Fresh Corn

When cutting fresh corn from the cob, a good trick is to use an upside-down Bundt pan. Stand the shucked ear of corn upright, with the tip placed in the center hole of the pan. Holding the cob steady, use a sharp knife and make long, downward strokes to remove the kernels.

Carnitas Tacos with Roasted Tomatillos

Recipe by Chef Scott Leibfried

For the Taco Challenge, Chef Scott competed against Chef Daniel to re-create a family's favorite carnitas tacos, which were made with slow-cooked pork ribs that were then shredded and fried. Kind of like a Mexican version of Southern pulled pork, the bits of meat are crisped in sizzling rendered pork fat. The original recipe clocked in at more than 1,500 calories and 127 grams of fat—that's more than twice the amount of fat you should consume in one day! Chef Scott rehabbed the pork by using pork loin chops, which are relatively lean but still have a great flavor and texture. Braising the chops in lime juice, broth, and piquant spices infuses the meat with zesty flavor and succulent moisture.

SERVES 4

PORK:

2 tablespoons smoked paprika

1 tablespoon granulated onion

½ teaspoon kosher salt

½ teaspoon freshly ground black pepper

2 (8-ounce) center rib pork loin chops, deboned, pounded

1 teaspoon canola oil

½ cup low-sodium chicken broth

Juice and finely grated zest of 4 limes

4 garlic cloves, minced

2 jalapeños, halved, seeded, and minced

2 tablespoons agave nectar

FOR SERVING:

2 tomatillos, halved crosswise

2 jalapeños, halved lengthwise, seeded if desired

2 limes, cut into wedges

8 corn tortillas

1 small onion, finely chopped

½ avocado, pitted, peeled, and thinly sliced

¼ cup chopped fresh cilantro leaves

To make the pork, in a small bowl combine the paprika, granulated onion, salt, and pepper. Mix with your fingers to evenly blend the spices. Put the pork chops on a large plate and sprinkle the spice mixture onto the meat to evenly coat all sides. If you have time, cover and refrigerate the pork chops for 1 hour or even overnight, to let the flavors sink in.

Put a large, wide Dutch oven or pot over medium-high heat and coat with the oil. When the oil is hot, lay the seasoned pork chops in the pot. Brown well on both sides, turning with tongs.

Pour in the chicken broth and scrape the bottom of the pot to release any browned bits of pork. Add the lime juice and zest, garlic, jalapeños, and agave nectar. Stir everything together and bring to a boil. Cover the pot and reduce the heat to medium-low. Simmer for 30 minutes, basting the pork with the liquid periodically. Remove the lid, turn the pork chops over with tongs, and continue to cook, covered, for 10 minutes. While the pork is cooking, make the taco accompaniments.

Put a grill pan or dry cast-iron skillet over high heat. Lay the tomatillos, jalapeños, and limes in the hot pan and cook until charred on all sides, turning with tongs. The limes will brown the quickest; remove to a side plate as they become ready. Once the skin of the tomatillos and jalapeños begins to crack and soften, transfer to a cutting board. Chop the tomatillos and slice the jalapeños for serving. Finally, lay the tortillas in the dry pan and brown lightly on both sides.

To serve, slice the pork chops into thin strips against the grain. Divide the meat among the corn tortillas. Top each taco with tomatillos, jalapeño, onion, avocado, and cilantro. Serve with the charred lime wedges.

Per serving: 393 calories, 12 g total fat (3 g saturated), 63 mg cholesterol, 344 mg sodium, 30 g protein, 7 g fiber, 45 g carb

Crispy Beef Tacos

Recipe by Chef Daniel Green

Chef Daniel's answer to the Taco Challenge was to not only swap pork for beef but also to make his own taco shells from soft corn tortillas. Those hard taco shells that come in a box at the grocery store not only are full of fat, sodium, and preservatives; they also crack as soon as you try to stuff them. When you make your own taco shells at home, they're healthier, tastier, and easier to work with. Chef Daniel's tip for a great-tasting and nutritious taco? "The best tacos get their flavor from the right blend of seasonings, not lots of salt or fat."

SERVES 4

TACOS:

8 corn tortillas

Nonstick cooking spray

1 tablespoon olive oil

1 small red onion, chopped

2 garlic cloves, minced

¾ pound 90% lean ground beef

¼ teaspoon kosher salt

¼ teaspoon freshly ground black pepper

1 tablespoon sun-dried tomato paste

1 teaspoon red pepper flakes

1 teaspoon dried oregano

½ teaspoon ground cumin

1 (8-ounce) can low-sodium tomato sauce

½ cup fresh cilantro, coarsely chopped

4 scallions, white and green parts, chopped

TOPPINGS:

2 cups shredded lettuce

½ cup reduced-fat shredded cheddar cheese

1 jalapeño, halved lengthwise, seeded if desired, and sliced

¼ cup fat-free sour cream

Preheat the oven to 300°F. Wrap the tortillas in damp paper towels and microwave on high for 30 seconds, until pliable. Discard the paper towels and coat the tortillas with nonstick spray. Fold the tortillas over the lip of a 13-by-9-inch baking dish with handles. Bake until crisp and firm, about 15 minutes.

In a large nonstick skillet, heat the olive oil over medium heat. When the oil is hot, add the onion and garlic. Cook and stir for a few minutes, until soft. Add the beef, breaking the meat up with the back of a spoon, until cooked through, 4 to 5 minutes. Season with salt and pepper.

Add the sun-dried tomato paste, red pepper flakes, oregano, and cumin, stirring to combine. Stir in the tomato sauce. Cook for another 5 minutes, until the mixture is thick. Remove from the heat and add the cilantro and scallions.

To serve, spoon a couple of tablespoons of the meat mixture in a taco shell. Top with lettuce, cheese, jalapeño, and sour cream.

Per serving (2 tacos): 429 calories, 18 g total fat (6 g saturated), 67 mg cholesterol, 461 mg sodium, 26 g protein, 5 g fiber, 42 g carb

Turkey and Cheese Enchiladas

Recipe by Chef Jaden Hair

Chef Jaden was daunted by the challenge of rehabbing a family's treasured enchilada recipe that had been passed down on the father's side for generations. Chef Jaden wanted to give this family, with its long-standing tradition of cooking meals together, a recipe that would continue to bring them together in the kitchen and stand the test of time. To do that, she cut back on the amount of cheese and added lean ground turkey. She also nixed frying altogether and swapped out some of the grated cheese for part-skim ricotta, which really lightens up the dish. All in all, Chef Jaden's changes amounted to a savings of more than 700 calories—and a recipe that everyone can feel good about passing down to future generations.

SERVES 6

SAUCE:

2 teaspoons olive oil

1 tablespoon whole wheat flour

2 cups low-sodium chicken broth

1 (8-ounce) can low-sodium tomato sauce

1 teaspoon chili powder

1 teaspoon chipotle chile powder

1 teaspoon granulated garlic

½ teaspoon ground cumin

ENCHILADAS:

2 teaspoons olive oil

½ onion, diced

1 garlic clove, minced

½ pound lean ground turkey breast, such as Jennie-O® Lean Ground Turkey

½ teaspoon kosher salt

¼ teaspoon freshly ground black pepper

½ teaspoon ground cumin

¾ cup part-skim ricotta cheese

12 corn tortillas

1 cup fat-free shredded mozzarella cheese

FOR SERVING:

2 large tomatoes, diced

Juice of ½ lime

2 tablespoons canned diced green chiles

1 tablespoon finely chopped fresh cilantro

4 tablespoons nonfat plain Greek yogurt

To make the enchilada sauce, put a pot over medium heat. Add the oil and sprinkle in the flour. Cook, stirring constantly with a wooden spoon, to form a paste, for about 1 minute. Add the broth, tomato sauce, chili powder, chipotle powder, garlic, and cumin, stirring to combine. Reduce the heat to medium-low and gently simmer the sauce until thickened, about 10 minutes.

To make the enchiladas, preheat the oven to 350°F.

Put a skillet over medium-high heat and coat with the oil. When the oil is hot, add the onion and garlic. Cook and stir until the onion and garlic begin to soften, about 2 minutes. Add the ground turkey and season with salt, pepper, and cumin. Cook the turkey until no longer pink, breaking it up with the back of a wooden spoon, about 7 to 10 minutes. Transfer the turkey mixture to a mixing bowl and stir in the ricotta cheese. Wipe out the skillet with a paper towel and return it to the heat.

Lay 1 tortilla in the hot pan. Cook for 10 seconds, until it puffs up. Using a spatula, lift up the tortilla and slide another one underneath it. As the tortillas brown, continue adding fresh tortillas underneath the cooked ones to keep them warm.

Spoon ½ cup of the enchilada sauce into a 9-by-13-inch baking dish. Working one at a time, dip the toasted tortillas in the remaining enchilada sauce to coat. Fill each tortilla with 2 tablespoons of the turkey filling and roll it up. Put the filled tortilla in the baking pan, seam side down. Continue until all of the tortillas are filled and rolled. Spread the remaining sauce over the top of the enchiladas, making sure all are covered with the sauce. Sprinkle the mozzarella on top. Bake until the cheese melts, 10 to 15 minutes.

In the meantime, in a bowl combine the tomatoes, lime juice, chiles, and cilantro to make a salsa.

Remove the enchiladas from the oven and allow to sit for 5 minutes. Scoop out 2 enchiladas per plate and top with a spoonful of the salsa and a dollop of yogurt.

Per serving (2 enchiladas): 304 calories, 10 g total fat (3 g saturated), 46 mg cholesterol, 454 mg sodium, 23 g protein, 5 g fiber, 34 g carb

Chinese Beef and Broccoli

Recipe by Chef Govind Armstrong

Chinese food is a takeout favorite for many families, but it can be tough to find healthy choices on most delivery menus. From heavy sauces rich in sugar and sodium to deep-fried meats to mounds of white rice—there aren't many options when you're looking for a nutritious meal. This rehabbed version of a popular restaurant dish slashes the sodium by cutting back on the sauce and uses flavorful, aromatic spices like ginger and garlic to re-create that authentic "Chinese takeout" flavor. Broccoli rabe and bok choy bulk up the stir-fry and add fiber and a wealth of vitamins and minerals. If you can't find broccoli rabe at the grocery store, you can substitute regular broccoli florets.

SERVES 4

- 3 tablespoons reduced-sodium soy sauce
- 1 tablespoon plus 1 teaspoon cornstarch
- Juice of 1 lime
- ¼ teaspoon red pepper flakes
- ½ pound top sirloin steak, preferably certified Angus beef, trimmed and sliced ⅛-inch thick, against the grain
- 1 pound broccoli rabe, ends trimmed
- ¼ cup low-sodium chicken broth
- 1 teaspoon light brown sugar
- 1 teaspoon sesame oil
- 2 tablespoons vegetable oil
- 4 scallions, white and green parts, chopped
- 4 garlic cloves, minced
- 1 tablespoon peeled and minced fresh ginger
- 4 heads baby bok choy, halved lengthwise and cut crosswise into 1-inch pieces
- 1 red bell pepper, halved, cored, seeded, and thinly sliced
- Chopped fresh cilantro, for garnish

In a small bowl, combine 2 tablespoons of the soy sauce, 1 tablespoon of the cornstarch, lime juice, and red pepper flakes. Mix with a spoon to dissolve the cornstarch. Put the steak in a baking pan, pour the marinade over the meat, toss to coat, and set aside.

To prepare the broccoli, bring a pot of water to a boil. Have ready a bowl filled with water and ice.

Cut the broccoli into bite-size pieces and cook it in the boiling water for about 1 minute. Drain and shock the broccoli in the ice water to stop the cooking process. Once the broccoli is completely cool, drain from the ice water, pat dry with paper towels, and set aside.

To make the sauce, in a small bowl combine the broth, remaining 1 tablespoon of soy sauce, remaining 1 teaspoon of cornstarch, sugar, and sesame oil. Mix with a spoon to dissolve the cornstarch. Set aside.

To prepare the stir-fry, put a wok over medium-high heat and coat with 1 tablespoon of the vegetable oil. Remove the beef from the marinade. Working in batches, stir-fry a few pieces of the beef until medium rare, 1 to 2 minutes, tossing constantly. Remove the cooked beef to a side dish and repeat with the remaining slices. Keep the wok on the heat.

Coat the wok with the remaining 1 tablespoon of vegetable oil. When the oil is hot, add the scallions, garlic, ginger, bok choy, and bell pepper. Cook, stirring, until the vegetables become tender, about 3 minutes. Add the blanched broccoli, tossing to incorporate. Return the beef to the wok and pour in the sauce, tossing to coat. Cook for 1 minute, until the sauce is thick.

Transfer the beef and vegetables to a serving platter. Garnish with cilantro and serve.

To watch a how-to video for this recipe, check out www.RecipeRehab.com.

Per serving: 253 calories, 12 g total fat (2.5 g saturated), 36 mg cholesterol, 537 mg sodium, 19 g protein, 5 g fiber, 21 g carb

Miso Salmon

Salmon is a fish commonly found on Japanese restaurant menus, and while salmon itself offers a host of nutritional benefits, the preparation of the fish can make or break the overall healthiness of the meal. This delicate miso salmon dish creates a perfect harmony of salty, sweet, rich, and acidic flavors. A touch of sesame oil provides nuttiness, while fresh orange juice unlocks the salmon's flavor, and miso adds a richness that rounds out the dish. And best of all, it takes only 30 minutes to pull together this elegant meal.

SERVES 4

¼ cup white miso (fermented soybean paste)

Juice of 1 orange (about ½ cup)

2 tablespoons unseasoned rice vinegar

½ cup low-sodium vegetable broth

1 tablespoon sesame oil

1 tablespoon light brown sugar, packed

1 scallion, white and green parts, thinly sliced

2 garlic cloves, minced

2 teaspoons peeled and minced fresh ginger

¼ teaspoon kosher salt

¼ teaspoon cayenne pepper

4 (5-ounce) salmon fillets, skin removed (see note, below)

In a small bowl, whisk together the miso, orange juice, vinegar, broth, sesame oil, sugar, scallion, garlic, ginger, salt, and cayenne. Once combined, divide into two bowls. Place the salmon in a single layer in a baking dish or container. Pour half of the miso marinade over the fish and turn to coat. Cover and chill for at least 30 minutes or up to 2 hours.

Preheat the broiler. Line a baking pan with aluminum foil. Remove the salmon fillets from the miso marinade and place side by side in the baking pan.

Pour the other half of the miso marinade into a small pot and place over medium heat. Simmer the marinade until reduced down by half into a sauce, about 2 minutes. Broil the salmon until the top is opaque and the center is pink, about 8 minutes. Drizzle the miso sauce over the salmon before serving.

Per serving: 327 calories, 14 g total fat (2 g saturated), 90 mg cholesterol, 681 mg sodium, 34 g protein, 7 g fiber, 14 g carb

Chef Tip: Salmon

From salads to stir-fries, salmon is a versatile fish that you can use in a wide variety of recipes. When buying salmon, look for wild-caught instead of farm-raised. It's a little bit more expensive, but wild-caught salmon contains higher levels of many nutrients and, unlike farmed salmon, doesn't contain high levels of toxic pollutants like PCBs. Most chefs would agree that wild-caught salmon also just plain tastes better!

Shredded Wheat–Crusted Fish and Chips with Tartar Sauce

Recipe by Chef Jill Davie

This much-beloved British pub dish is typically made with cod that's been dipped in a thick, eggy batter and deep-fried, then served alongside fried potato wedges—not exactly a healthy family meal. Chef Jill wanted to keep that crunchy coating on the fish, but instead of coating it in a heavy batter and frying it, she dipped the cod in egg whites and then gently rolled each piece in shredded wheat before baking to golden-brown perfection. The "chips" have also been lightened up by using skin-on fingerling potatoes, which are even more delicious than the deep-fried version—you'll make these crispy yet tender potatoes time and again. A tangy homemade tartar sauce with fresh lemon is the perfect accompaniment to this rehabbed "pub grub."

SERVES 4

FISH:

Nonstick cooking spray

½ cup all-purpose flour

2 teaspoons Old Bay Seasoning

4 large egg whites

6 shredded wheat biscuits

2 pounds fresh cod fillets or any firm white fish, cut into strips

CHIPS:

1 pound fingerling potatoes, scrubbed

2 tablespoons olive oil

2 teaspoons dried oregano

1 teaspoon granulated garlic

¼ teaspoon kosher salt

¼ teaspoon freshly ground black pepper

SAUCE:

1 cup fat-free sour cream

2 tablespoons chopped fresh chives

Juice and finely grated zest of 1 lemon

Pinch cayenne pepper

Preheat the oven to 400°F. Coat a baking pan with nonstick spray.

Spread the flour on a flat plate and season with Old Bay. In a shallow bowl, whisk the egg whites. Crush the wheat biscuits and put on another flat plate.

Working with one piece at a time, dredge pieces of fish in the flour, shaking off the excess. Dip the fish in the egg whites, allowing the excess to drip back into the bowl. Coat all sides of the fish in the shredded wheat, pressing to adhere.

Lay the fish pieces side by side on the prepared baking pan; spray the tops with nonstick spray. Bake for 10 minutes, until the fish is flaky and the crust is crisp and golden brown.

To make the chips, put the fingerlings in a pot of salted cool water and bring to a boil over medium-high heat. Simmer until the potatoes are fork-tender, about 20 minutes. Drain the potatoes and set aside until cool enough to handle. Cut the potatoes in half lengthwise.

Put a cast-iron skillet over medium-high heat and coat with the oil. When the oil is hot, lay the potatoes in the pan, cut side down, in a single layer. (You may have to do this in batches.) Sear the potatoes for 5 to 7 minutes, until crisp and brown. Sprinkle the potatoes with oregano and garlic and season with salt and pepper.

To make the sauce, in a small bowl mix together the sour cream, chives, lemon juice, zest, and cayenne. Stir with a spoon.

Divide the fish and potatoes onto 4 plates and serve immediately, with tartar sauce on the side.

Per serving: 579 calories, 10 g total fat (2 g saturated), 103 mg cholesterol, 672 mg sodium, 54 g protein, 7 g fiber, 67 g carb

Lightened-Up Bacon Cheeseburger Pizza

Recipe by Chef Jet Tila

What do you get when you combine two of America's favorite junk foods—bacon cheeseburgers and pizza? Usually, you get a high-calorie nutritional nightmare. But Chef Jet didn't disappoint when he rehabbed a family's favorite pizza recipe. Made with lean ground beef and all of your favorite fixings, this indulgent dish is sure to satisfy multiple cravings, whether you're dying for the drive-through or the pizza joint.

SERVES 4

Nonstick cooking spray

12 ounces prepared pizza dough

½ pound 90 percent lean ground beef

1 onion, halved and thinly sliced

¼ teaspoon kosher salt

½ teaspoon freshly ground black pepper

½ cup no-salt-added ketchup

1 tablespoon yellow mustard

2 slices cooked bacon, crumbled

½ cup reduced-fat shredded cheddar cheese

1 cup shredded iceberg lettuce

1 tomato, chopped

Preheat the oven to 400°F. Coat a large baking pan with nonstick spray. Press the dough onto the baking pan; starting at the center, stretch it to reach the sides of the pan.

Coat a large nonstick skillet with cooking spray and place over medium-high heat. When the pan is hot, add the beef and onion; cook and stir until the beef is browned and the onion is soft, about 10 minutes. Season with salt and pepper. Tip out and discard any fat or liquid in the bottom of the pan.

Stir in ketchup and mustard until fully incorporated into the meat. Spoon the meat mixture evenly over the pizza dough. Sprinkle with the crumbled bacon and shredded cheese.

Bake the pizza for about 15 minutes or until the crust is golden brown and the cheese is melted. Top with lettuce and tomato. Cut the pizza into squares. Serve immediately.

Per serving : 421 calories, 15 g total fat (5 g saturated), 51 mg cholesterol, 680 mg sodium, 23 g protein, 2 g fiber, 53 g carb

Southern-Style Drumsticks with Corn Muffins, page 101

Part 5

QUICK
CHICKEN

Pulled Barbecue Chicken Sandwiches

Recipe by Chef Laura Vitale

Chef Laura rehabbed a family's indulgent pulled pork sandwich recipe by focusing on developing flavor through an inventive cooking technique. Swapping chicken for pork, she used bone-in, skin-on chicken breasts, which are full of flavor and moisture, and simply discarded the skin and bone after cooking. When combined with her homemade barbecue sauce, the tender shredded chicken takes on a sweet smokiness that's far better than anything you could find in a bottle at the grocery store.

SERVES 6 (MAKES 12 SANDWICHES)

CHICKEN:

Nonstick cooking spray

3 pounds bone-in, skin-on chicken breast halves

1 tablespoon olive oil

½ teaspoon freshly ground black pepper

SAUCE:

1 tablespoon olive oil

1 small onion, finely chopped

2 garlic cloves, minced

2 tablespoons tomato paste

1 tablespoon apple cider vinegar

½ cup low-sodium tomato puree

¼ cup no-salt-added ketchup

1 tablespoon Worcestershire sauce

1 tablespoon Splenda Brown Sugar Blend

1 tablespoon paprika

1 tablespoon dry mustard

1 teaspoon chili powder

½ cup water

12 (1½-ounce) slider burger buns

To make the chicken, preheat the oven to 375°F. Line a baking pan with aluminum foil and coat with nonstick spray.

Arrange the chicken breasts side by side in the prepared baking pan and drizzle the olive oil all over the top; season with pepper. Bake the chicken until barely pink in the center, about 40 minutes.

To make the sauce, put a pot over medium heat and coat with the oil. When the oil is hot, add the onion and garlic. Cook, stirring, until soft and fragrant, 2 to 3 minutes. Stir in the tomato paste until fully incorporated. Stir in the vinegar, loosening up any brown bits on the bottom of the pan.

Add the tomato puree, ketchup, Worcestershire, sugar blend, paprika, mustard, chili powder, and water. Bring the barbecue sauce to a simmer, stirring, and then reduce the heat to low and simmer gently for 20 minutes, until the sauce is slightly thickened.

Allow the cooked chicken to cool slightly, then peel off and discard the skin. Using 2 forks, shred the meat and discard the bone.

Add the shredded chicken to the sauce and stir to incorporate. Simmer for another 5 minutes, until the chicken has soaked up the sauce and is heated through. Divide the chicken among the buns and serve.

Per serving (2 sandwiches): 510 calories, 13 g total fat (2 g saturated), 94 mg cholesterol, 722 mg sodium, 41 g protein, 4 g fiber, 56 g carb

Shepherd's Pie with Chicken

Recipe by Chef Jill Davie

Shepherd's pie is the ultimate meat-and-potatoes meal. It's classically hearty, stick-to-your-ribs kind of food, and chances are any fans of the dish want to keep it that way. So with that in mind, Chef Jill lightened up a family's much-loved recipe without losing any of the comforting flavor. She swapped out ground beef for lean ground chicken, and instead of topping the pie with regular mashed potatoes, she used sweet potatoes, which are lower on the glycemic index and contain more nutrients than white potatoes. This recipe takes a little bit of time to prepare, but the results are worth it. Leftovers are also a plus—this dish is just as delicious reheated on the second day.

SERVES 6

TOPPING:

- 1½ pounds sweet potatoes, peeled and cut into 2-inch pieces
- 2 tablespoons unsweetened plain almond milk
- 2 tablespoons lemon juice
- ¼ teaspoon kosher salt
- ¼ teaspoon freshly ground black pepper

FILLING:

- 1 tablespoon vegetable oil
- 1 small onion, finely chopped
- 1 celery stalk, finely chopped
- 1 carrot, finely chopped
- 2 garlic cloves, minced
- 2 tablespoons chopped fresh oregano
- 2 teaspoons chopped fresh thyme
- 1 teaspoon chopped fresh rosemary
- 1 pound 93% lean ground chicken or turkey
- Pinch kosher salt
- ¼ teaspoon freshly ground black pepper
- 1 (15-ounce) can low-sodium crushed tomatoes
- ¼ pound green beans, trimmed and cut into ½-inch pieces
- 1 zucchini, chopped

To make the topping, put the cut sweet potatoes into a large pot of salted cool water to cover. Bring to a boil over medium-high heat. Reduce the heat to medium and then simmer until the potatoes are fork tender, about 20 to 25 minutes. Drain the sweet potatoes well in a colander and transfer to a mixing bowl. While the potatoes are still warm, mash with a potato masher or a handheld mixer. Add in the almond milk and mix until it's incorporated and the sweet potatoes are fluffy. Stir in lemon juice. Season with salt and pepper. Cover and keep warm.

Preheat the oven to 350°F.

Coat a large nonstick skillet with the oil and put over medium heat. When the oil is hot, add the onion, celery, carrot, and garlic. Stir in the oregano, thyme, and rosemary. Cook, stirring occasionally, for 6 to 7 minutes, until the vegetables soften.

Add the ground chicken, breaking up the clumps with the back of a wooden spoon; season with salt and pepper. Continue to sauté until the meat is cooked through and most of the excess liquid has evaporated, about 10 minutes.

Pour in the tomatoes and bring to a simmer. Mix in the green beans and zucchini.

To assemble, ladle the chicken-and-vegetable mixture into the bottom of an 8-by-8-inch casserole dish. Spread the mashed sweet potatoes evenly on top of the casserole.

Bake until the potatoes begin to brown and the meat is heated through, about 30 minutes. Spoon onto plates and serve immediately.

Per serving: 283 calories, 8 g total fat (2 g saturated), 54 mg cholesterol, 257 mg sodium, 18 g protein, 6 g fiber, 32 g carb

REHAB TIP: SWEET POTATOES As with carrots, the bright orange hue of sweet potatoes signals that they are rich in beta-carotene, an A vitamin that helps to promote healthy eyesight and protect against heart disease. Sweet potatoes also contain more fiber than white potatoes. You can swap out white potatoes for sweet potatoes in almost any recipe for a similar dish that contains more nutrients.

Better-Than-Takeout Orange Chicken

Recipe by Chef Jill Davie

In about the time it takes to order and pick up Chinese takeout, you can make this delicious, much healthier version of orange chicken. Chef Jill rehabbed this recipe using a combination of orange juice and orange marmalade spiked with chili sauce to create a tangy, spicy, and totally addictive sauce. She also swapped out white rice for brown rice, which has more fiber and adds a nice texture to the dish. Chef Jill's orange sauce is also delicious on seafood—try brushing it on grilled shrimp or salmon to add instant Asian flavor to any meal.

SERVES 4

SAUCE:

⅔ cup orange juice

⅓ cup store-bought natural orange marmalade

1 teaspoon chili paste

2 tablespoons dry sherry or white wine

1 tablespoon reduced-sodium soy sauce

2 teaspoons sesame seeds

CHICKEN:

1½ pounds skinless, boneless chicken breast halves, cut into chunks

3 tablespoons cornstarch

1 tablespoon canola oil

1 tablespoon peeled and minced fresh ginger

2 garlic cloves, minced

2 scallions, white and green parts, thinly sliced

½ red bell pepper, cored and thinly sliced

1 cup cooked brown rice, for serving

To make the sauce, in a pot over medium heat, combine the orange juice, marmalade, chili sauce, sherry or white wine, soy sauce, and sesame seeds. Gently simmer, stirring occasionally, for 5 to 7 minutes, until thick enough to coat the back of a spoon. Cover the orange sauce and keep warm.

Pat the chicken chunks dry with paper towels and toss with the cornstarch.

Put a large skillet over high heat and coat with the oil. When the oil is hot, add the chicken in batches so you don't overcrowd the pan. Stir-fry the chicken for 5 to 7 minutes, until lightly browned.

Remove the chicken to a side platter as it becomes cooked.

To the skillet drippings, add the ginger, garlic, and scallions. Cook and stir for 1 minute, until fragrant. Add the bell pepper and stir-fry for about 2 minutes, until softened. Return the chicken to the pan, along with any accumulated juices on the platter. Add the orange sauce, tossing the chicken to coat. Serve the orange chicken over brown rice.

Per serving: 413 calories, 9 g total fat (1 g saturated), 109 mg cholesterol, 378 mg sodium, 39 g protein, 2 g fiber, 42 g carb

Light Chicken Parmesan with Sausage-Tomato Sauce

Recipe by Chef Laura Vitale

Who doesn't love Chicken Parmesan? Fried chicken smothered in cheese, served with pasta and tomato sauce—it's a delicious indulgence that's also a nutritional nightmare. When Chef Laura was tasked with making over a family's Chicken Parmesan recipe, she knew she could make a mouthwatering alternative with a few easy changes. Two simple substitutions—using whole wheat versions of bread crumbs and pasta—increase the fiber, and soaking lean turkey sausage in red wine before adding it to the tomato sauce creates rich layers of flavor without a lot of added fat. All in all, her rehabbed recipe reduced the amount of calories by more than half and cut the fat by 80 percent.

SERVES 4

SAUCE:

1 (2-ounce) link lean hot Italian turkey sausage, such as Jennie-O® Lean Hot Italian Turkey Sausage

½ cup dry red wine, such as Cabernet Sauvignon

1 teaspoon olive oil

1 yellow onion, finely chopped

2 garlic cloves, minced

½ teaspoon fennel seeds, crushed with the back of a skillet

Pinch kosher salt

½ teaspoon freshly ground black pepper

1 (28-ounce) can organic crushed tomatoes

4 fresh basil leaves, hand-torn, plus more for garnish

CHICKEN PARMESAN:

4 (4-ounce) boneless, skinless chicken breast halves, pounded thin

1 teaspoon Italian seasoning

Pinch teaspoon kosher salt

¼ teaspoon freshly ground black pepper

1 teaspoon olive oil

½ cup shredded reduced-fat mozzarella cheese

¼ cup of whole wheat panko (Japanese-style bread crumbs)

3 tablespoons grated Parmesan cheese

½ pound whole wheat angel-hair pasta, cooked al dente, for serving

To prepare the sauce, remove the sausage casings and crumble the meat into a large bowl. Pour the wine over the sausage and mix with your fingers so the sausage is evenly moistened.

Put a pot over medium heat and coat with the oil. When the oil is hot, add the onion. Cook and stir until the onion begins to soften, about 5 minutes. Stir in the garlic, fennel seeds, salt, and pepper. When everything is sizzling, add the sausage, along with any wine remaining in the bowl. Cook, stirring, until the wine cooks away and the sausage becomes browned and is no longer pink, about 10 minutes. Pour in the tomatoes and add the basil. Simmer the sauce for 20 minutes, stirring occasionally.

To prepare the chicken, preheat the oven to 400°F.

Season the chicken breasts with Italian seasoning, salt, and pepper. Coat a large ovenproof skillet with the oil and put over medium heat. Sear the chicken for about 3 minutes on each side (it will cook very quickly).

Leaving the chicken in the skillet, top each breast with a ladleful of sauce and sprinkle the top evenly with the shredded mozzarella. In a small bowl, combine the bread crumbs and Parmesan cheese and sprinkle all over the top.

Transfer the pan to the oven. Bake until the cheese is bubbly, about 10 minutes.

To serve, toss the cooked angel-hair with a ladleful of the tomato sauce. Divide the pasta among four plates. Top with a portion of chicken Parmesan and garnish with fresh basil.

Per serving: 539 calories, 9 g total fat (2 g saturated), 84 mg cholesterol, 462 mg sodium, 45 g protein, 10 g fiber, 61 g carb

Herbed Chicken Parmesan with Roasted Tomato Sauce

Recipe by Chef Scott Leibfried

When Chef Scott set about rehabbing Chicken Parm, the pasta was the first thing to go. In his own words: "Who says you need a huge bowl of pasta with Chicken Parmesan? It just makes you want to take a nap." By cutting out the pasta, he reduced the carbohydrates in the original recipe by 80 percent. Chef Scott also cut out the jarred marinara sauce and created his own fresh, chunky sauce, using oven-roasted cherry tomatoes. And instead of adding mounds of shredded mozzarella, he used just four slices of reduced-fat mozzarella to fully cover the chicken with melted cheese and achieve that stringy, gooey experience when you cut into it and take your first bite.

SERVES 4

SAUCE:

2 pints cherry tomatoes, halved crosswise

¼ small red onion, thinly sliced

2 garlic cloves, minced

2 tablespoons balsamic vinegar

1 tablespoon olive oil

4 large fresh basil leaves, chopped

¼ teaspoon kosher salt

¼ teaspoon freshly ground black pepper

CHICKEN PARMESAN:

1 cup whole wheat panko (Japanese-style bread crumbs)

2 tablespoons coarsely chopped fresh flat-leaf parsley

1 teaspoon fresh thyme leaves

1 teaspoon finely grated fresh lemon zest

1½ teaspoons granulated garlic

1½ teaspoons granulated onion

4 large egg whites, beaten with 1 tablespoon water

4 (4-ounce) boneless, skinless chicken breasts, pounded to ¼-inch thick

2 teaspoons olive oil

4 slices reduced-fat mozzarella cheese

¼ cup grated Parmesan cheese

4 large fresh basil leaves, chopped

To make the tomato sauce, preheat the oven to 375°F.

In a large mixing bowl, combine the tomatoes, onion, garlic, vinegar, oil, basil, salt, and pepper, tossing to coat. Spread the tomato mixture on a nonstick baking pan. Bake until the tomatoes have shriveled a bit and the skins begin to pull away, about 25 minutes.

To make the chicken, put the bread crumbs in a food processor and add the parsley, thyme, lemon zest, and garlic and onion powders. Pulse until the mixture is finely ground. Set up an assembly line for the breading process: a shallow dish with beaten egg white and water, then a plate with the bread crumbs.

Working with 1 piece of chicken at a time, dip the chicken into the beaten egg whites, letting the excess drip back into the bowl. Coat the chicken with the bread-crumb mixture, gently pressing in the crumbs. Set aside on a large plate and continue with the remaining chicken.

Put a large nonstick skillet over medium-high heat and coat with the oil. When the oil is hot, cook the chicken for 3 to 4 minutes on each side, until golden brown. You may have to do this in batches.

Remove the roasted tomatoes from the oven. Put half of the mixture in a food processor and puree until smooth; reserve the remaining roasted tomatoes in a bowl for garnish.

Using the same baking pan, arrange the seared chicken breasts in a single layer. Top each with a slice of mozzarella and a sprinkle of Parmesan. Bake the chicken until the cheese is melted, about 5 minutes.

To serve, pool the pureed tomato sauce on the bottom of each plate. Cut the chicken breasts diagonally into 1-inch slices and shingle the slices over the sauce. Top with the reserved roasted tomatoes and fresh basil.

Per serving: 386 calories, 13 g total fat (4 g saturated), 80 mg cholesterol, 502 mg sodium, 42 g protein, 4 g fiber, 25 g carb

REHAB TIP: PANKO   When a recipe calls for bread crumbs, swap them out for panko, or Japanese-style bread crumbs. They are flakier and crunchier than regular bread crumbs, so they not only add terrific texture to your favorite recipes but also absorb less oil than traditional bread crumbs.

Chicken Fried Farro

Recipe by Chef Spike Mendelsohn

Fried rice is typically little more than cooked rice, either white or brown, that's fried in a wok with oil, soy sauce, and maybe a few vegetables—it doesn't offer much nutritional value. Chef Spike rehabbed this recipe by adding chicken for some healthy protein and swapping out the rice for whole-grain farro. He also added vegetables like snow peas and zucchini to give color to the plate, volume to the dish, and, of course, nutrients to your body. The result is a well-rounded and satisfying dish that will fill you up for fewer than 400 calories.

SERVES 4

1 cup farro

2 tablespoons canola oil

½ pound skinless, boneless chicken breast, cut into small chunks

3 garlic cloves, minced

1-inch piece fresh ginger, peeled and minced

2 scallions, white and green parts, finely chopped

½ pound snow peas, cut on the diagonal

2 zucchini squash, green and yellow, chopped small

1 large egg, lightly beaten

2 tablespoons reduced-sodium soy sauce

To prepare the farro, bring a 2-quart pot of water to a boil. Add the farro, reduce the heat to medium-low, and cover. Simmer until tender and the grains have split open, about 20 minutes. Drain and rinse with cool water.

Coat a wok or large, wide skillet with 1 tablespoon of the oil and place over medium-high heat. When the oil is hot, add the chicken. Cook and stir for 3 minutes, until the chicken is cooked through. Scrape the chicken onto a side plate and return the wok to the heat.

Coat the wok with the remaining 1 tablespoon of oil. Add the garlic, ginger, and scallions; stir-fry for 30 seconds, until fragrant. Add the snow peas and squash. Cook, tossing the vegetables, until tender. Move the ingredients to the side of the pan and pour the egg into the center. Scramble the egg lightly, just until set but not brown. Return the chicken, along with any accumulated juices, to the pan, tossing quickly to incorporate. Fold in the cooked farro and toss to combine well.

Moisten the stir-fry with soy sauce. Toss the ingredients together until heated through. Spoon onto a serving platter or divide into four bowls and serve immediately.

Chef Tip: Farro

Farro is a wheat-derived grain that looks like a plumper version of brown rice and has an earthy, nutty flavor and a firm, chewy texture. With twice as much fiber and protein as white rice, it's a healthy and versatile choice for many recipes, including stir-fries.

To watch a how-to video for this recipe, check out www.RecipeRehab.com.

Per serving: 350 calories, 10 g total fat (1 g saturated), 78 mg cholesterol, 346 mg sodium, 23 g protein, 6 g fiber, 43 g carb

"Unfried Chicken" with Spicy Slaw

Recipe by Chef Spike Mendelsohn

When Chef Spike faced off against Chef Laura to rehab a family's beloved fried chicken recipe, his first order of business was to cut the fat content in half by swapping out the skin-on dark meat in the chicken legs and thighs for skinless, boneless chicken breasts. Then he coated the chicken with egg white, rolled it in cornmeal, and pan-seared it on the stovetop to create that distinctive crunchy exterior, before finishing it off in the oven to keep the meat moist and succulent. A refreshing and colorful vegetable slaw made with red and green cabbage complements this dish and adds a nice dose of vegetables to the plate.

SERVES 6

CHICKEN:

Nonstick cooking spray

½ cup whole wheat flour

4 large egg whites

1 cup cornmeal, such as Bob's Red Mill whole grain

2 tablespoons chopped fresh flat-leaf parsley

Finely grated zest of 1 lemon (about 2 teaspoons)

1 teaspoon granulated garlic

½ teaspoon coarse salt

¼ teaspoon freshly ground black pepper

6 skinless, boneless chicken breast halves (about 4 ounces each)

2 tablespoons vegetable oil

SLAW:

2 tablespoons light mayonnaise, such as Hellmann's/Best Foods

2 tablespoons apple cider vinegar

2 tablespoons hot sauce, such as Frank's RedHot

1½ teaspoons Creole mustard, such as Zatarain's

1 cup shredded green cabbage

1 cup shredded red cabbage

½ cup shredded carrot

1 cup sweet corn kernels, either fresh or frozen and thawed

½ small red onion, chopped

½ teaspoon coarse salt

¼ teaspoon freshly ground black pepper

To prepare the chicken, preheat the oven to 350°F. Coat a large baking pan with nonstick spray. Set aside.

Prepare a breading station: First, put the flour on a large plate. Pour the egg whites into a wide, shallow bowl and whisk until foamy. On a separate plate, combine the cornmeal, parsley, lemon zest, granulated garlic, salt, and pepper. Mix with a fork.

Put the chicken in between two pieces of wax paper or plastic wrap. Using a meat mallet or the bottom of a heavy pan, pound the chicken until ¼-inch thick. Working with one piece at a time, dredge the chicken in the flour, shaking off the excess; dip in the egg white; then dredge in the cornmeal mixture to coat both sides. Set the breaded chicken on a side platter.

Place a cast-iron skillet over medium heat and coat with the oil. When the oil is hot, add two pieces of the chicken; cook until browned on both sides, turning once, 3 to 5 minutes total. Remove the chicken from the skillet and set on the prepared baking pan. Repeat with the remaining chicken. Transfer the baking pan to the oven and bake until cooked through, about 15 minutes.

To prepare the slaw, in a small bowl mix the mayonnaise, vinegar, hot sauce, and mustard. Stir to blend the ingredients together. In a mixing bowl, combine the green and red cabbage, carrot, corn, and onion. Pour the mayonnaise dressing over the slaw and toss well to coat. Season with salt and pepper.

To serve, slice the chicken and divide among six plates. Serve with the slaw on the side.

Per serving: 345 calories, 12 g total fat (2 g saturated), 66 mg cholesterol, 675 mg sodium, 29 g protein, 6 g fiber, 30 g carb

Chef Tip

Deep-frying meat adds a tremendous amount of calories and fat. Most often, the taste and texture can be replicated by pan-frying and finishing the meat in the oven. A cast-iron skillet is a great tool for this technique, because cast iron distributes heat evenly and can go from stovetop to oven—and even to table—effortlessly.

Southern-Style Drumsticks with Corn Muffins

Recipe by Chef Laura Vitale

In Chef Laura's version of "fried" chicken, she kept the rich meat of the chicken legs but rehabbed the cooking method by coating the chicken in flour and spices before baking it in the oven. Her secret to creating the perfect skin is to place the coated legs in the refrigerator so that they dry out a little before baking—the skin really crisps up in the oven once the moisture has evaporated from its surface. True to southern tradition, Chef Laura serves her chicken with homemade corn muffins. Made with low-fat buttermilk and just a little bit of light butter, these corn muffins are sweet, moist, and fluffy.

SERVES 4

CHICKEN:

½ cup all-purpose flour

2 teaspoons baking powder

2 teaspoons granulated garlic

2 teaspoons granulated onion

1 teaspoon paprika

¼ teaspoon kosher salt

½ teaspoon freshly ground black pepper

8 skin-on chicken drumsticks

1 tablespoon vegetable oil

Hot sauce, for serving

MUFFINS:

1 cup all-purpose flour

3 tablespoons sugar

1 cup yellow cornmeal

1 tablespoon baking powder

1 teaspoons baking soda

¼ teaspoon salt

1 cup of low-fat buttermilk

1 large egg

1 large egg white

3 tablespoons light butter, such as Land O'Lakes, melted

To make the chicken, in a large resealable plastic bag add the flour, baking powder, garlic and onion powders, paprika, salt, and pepper. Seal the bag and shake it to mix the dry ingredients well. Add the drumsticks to the bag, seal again, and toss for about 1 minute to coat.

Set a wire rack insert inside a roasting pan. Remove the drumsticks from the bag, shaking off any excess flour. Arrange them on the baking rack and put them in the fridge for at least 45 minutes, uncovered, to dry out. (You can do this the night before.)

Remove the chicken from the fridge and let it come to room temperature for about 15 minutes. Meanwhile, preheat the oven to 400°F.

Drizzle 1½ teaspoons of the oil evenly over the top of the chicken legs and place them, still on the rack, in the oven. Bake for about 30 minutes. Using tongs, flip the chicken over and drizzle the remaining 1½ teaspoons of oil evenly all over them. Bake for another 20 to 25 minutes, until deep golden brown and crispy.

To make the muffins, preheat the oven to 375°F; line a standard 12-capacity muffin tin with liners and set aside.

In a large bowl, whisk together the flour, sugar, cornmeal, baking powder, baking soda, and salt. Set aside.

In a separate bowl, whisk the buttermilk, egg, egg white, and melted butter. Pour the wet mixture into the dry ingredients and mix everything together with a rubber spatula until you have a smooth batter.

Using an ice cream scoop, divide the batter into the prepared muffin tin.

Bake for 15 minutes or until a toothpick inserted into the center comes out clean. Serve the muffins with the chicken and hot sauce on the side, if desired.

CHICKEN:

Per serving: 335 calories, 16 g total fat (4 g saturated), 118 mg cholesterol, 510 mg sodium, 30 g protein, 1 g fiber, 15 g carb

CORN MUFFINS:

Per serving (one muffin): 127 calories, 2 g total fat (1 g saturated), 18 mg cholesterol, 331 mg sodium, 4 g protein, 1 g fiber, 23 g carb

General Tso's Chicken

Recipe by Chef Govind Armstrong

General Tso's chicken is a popular item at many Chinese restaurants. Made with chunks of deep-fried chicken and coated with a thick, sweet sauce, many versions of this dish clock in at well over 1,000 calories. When Chef Govind rehabbed this recipe for a family of die-hard General Tso's fans, he created a light marinade that allows the chicken to soak up extra flavor before pan-frying. Ready in 35 minutes, this rehabbed recipe is simple enough to prepare on a weeknight.

SERVES 4

MARINADE:

4 large egg whites

2 tablespoons low-sodium soy sauce

2 tablespoons sherry vinegar

½ teaspoon freshly ground black pepper

½ pound skinless, boneless chicken breast, cut into 1-inch cubes

SAUCE:

½ cup low-sodium chicken broth

1 tablespoon low-sodium soy sauce

1 tablespoon unseasoned rice vinegar

1 tablespoon hoisin sauce

1 teaspoon sesame oil

1 teaspoon cornstarch

STIR-FRY:

2 tablespoons vegetable oil

¼ cup cornstarch, for dusting

6 scallions, white and green parts, cut into 2-inch pieces

4 garlic cloves, minced

2 teaspoons peeled and minced fresh ginger

4 dried red chiles, smashed

1 head Napa cabbage, halved lengthwise then cut crosswise into ribbons

1 (15-ounce) can pineapple chunks in juice, drained

1 teaspoon sesame seeds, toasted

To prepare the marinade, whisk together the egg whites, soy sauce, vinegar, and black pepper in a mixing bowl. Add the chicken and marinate for 15 minutes.

To prepare the sauce, combine the broth, soy sauce, vinegar, hoisin sauce, sesame oil, and cornstarch in a mixing bowl. Whisk all of the ingredients together to dissolve the cornstarch.

To cook the chicken, put a wok over medium-high heat and coat with 1 tablespoon of the vegetable oil. Put the additional ¼ cup cornstarch in a bowl. Remove the chicken from the marinade and dust lightly in the cornstarch. Cook until the chicken is no longer pink, 3 to 4 minutes, tossing constantly. Remove the cooked chicken to a side platter. Keep the wok on the heat and coat with the remaining vegetable oil. Add the scallions, garlic, ginger, and chiles. Cook, stirring, until aromatic, about 30 seconds. Add the cabbage, then pour in the sauce and cook for about 1 minute to thicken. Return the chicken to the wok and add the pineapple. Toss thoroughly to coat in the sauce. Garnish with the sesame seeds and serve immediately.

Per serving: 287 calories, 10 g total fat (2 g saturated), 32 mg cholesterol, 423 mg sodium, 17 g protein, 3 g fiber, 32 g carb

Chicken Caesar Salad

When it comes to salads, looks can be deceiving. Caesar salads are particularly tricky, because they're often loaded with croutons and Parmesan cheese, then drenched with a rich dressing. This pared-down version contains all of the essential components of a great Caesar salad: crisp lettuce, real Parmesan, crusty cubes of toasted bread, and a dressing brightly flavored with garlic, lemon, and anchovy. Buttermilk and a little light mayo stand in for eggs and oil to create a creamy, tangy dressing.

SERVES 4 (MAKES 1 CUP DRESSING)

CROUTONS:

1 (4-ounce) French demi-baguette, crusts removed, cut into ½-inch cubes (about 2 cups)

Nonstick cooking spray

½ teaspoon granulated garlic

½ teaspoon dried oregano

Pinch kosher salt

¼ teaspoon cayenne pepper

DRESSING:

½ cup low-fat buttermilk

2 tablespoons light mayonnaise

Juice of ½ lemon

2 teaspoons red wine vinegar

2 teaspoons anchovy paste

1 teaspoon Dijon mustard

1 teaspoon Worcestershire sauce

2 dashes hot sauce, such as Tabasco

3 garlic cloves, minced

Pinch kosher salt

½ teaspoon freshly ground black pepper

2 tablespoons extra-virgin olive oil

SALAD:

2 romaine lettuce hearts, cored and chopped (about 5 cups)

8 ounces grilled skinless, boneless chicken breasts, cubed (about 2 cups)

¼ cup freshly grated Parmesan cheese

To prepare the croutons, preheat the oven to 350°F.

Put the bread cubes in a large bowl and spray with nonstick cooking spray; toss until coated. Sprinkle the granulated garlic, oregano, salt, and cayenne pepper over the bread cubes and toss until evenly coated. Spread the bread cubes in a baking pan in a single layer. Bake until the croutons are golden, about 15 minutes. Set aside to cool.

To make the dressing, in a blender combine the buttermilk, mayonnaise, lemon juice, vinegar, anchovy paste, mustard, Worcestershire, hot sauce, garlic, salt, and pepper. Puree until the dressing is smooth. Drizzle in the oil until incorporated.

To serve, put the lettuce in a salad bowl; add the chicken, croutons, and cheese. Add enough dressing to coat and toss gently to distribute. Serve immediately.

Per serving: 316 calories, 12 g total fat (2.5 g saturated), 61 mg cholesterol, 758 mg sodium, 26 g protein, 2 g fiber, 26 g carb

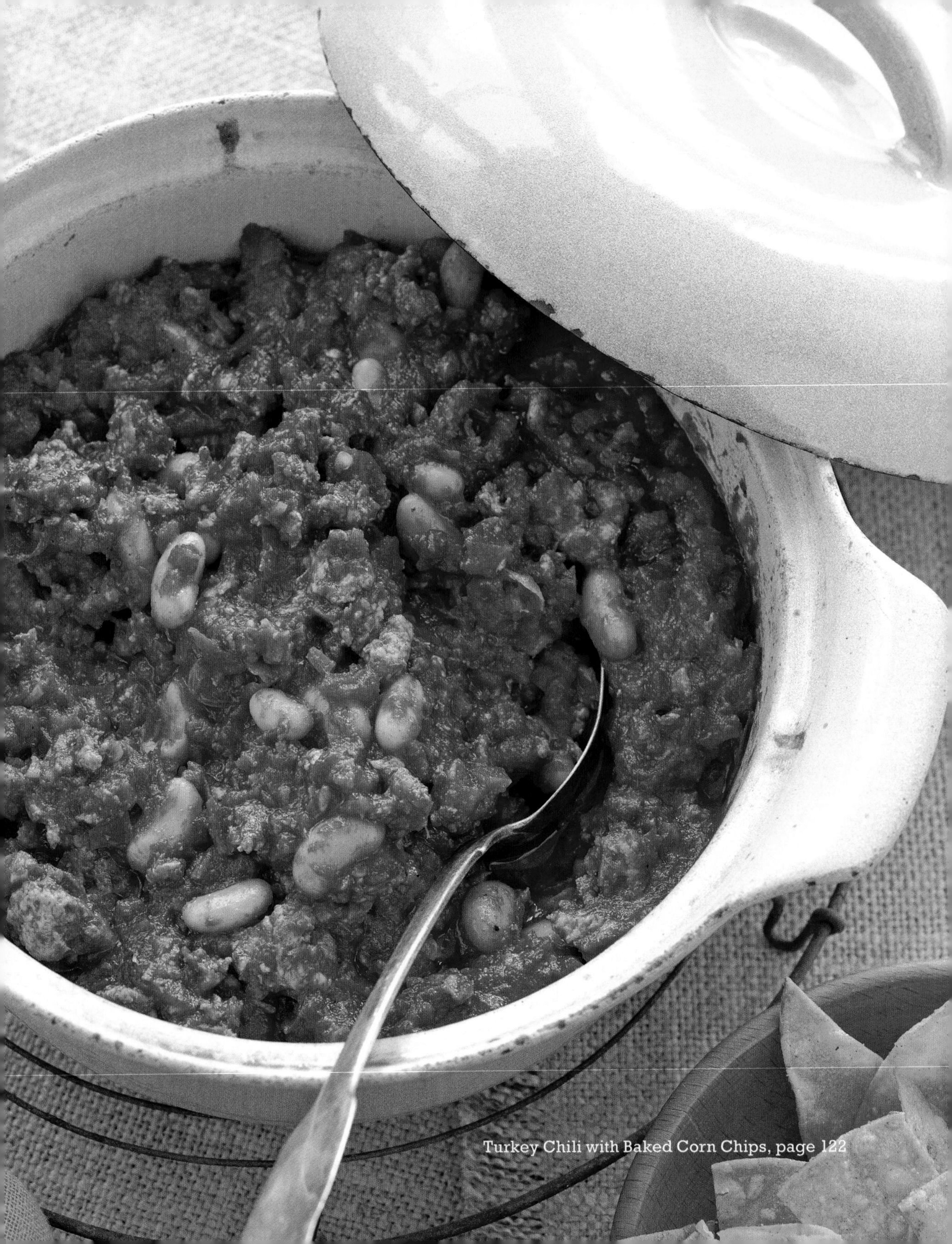

Turkey Chili with Baked Corn Chips, page 122

Part 6

FAMILY
FAVORITES

Country-Style Meatloaf

Recipe by Chef Daniel Green

There is no denying that meatloaf is the king of comfort food. The truth is, it's just as easy to make a healthy one as it is a fattening one. Most meatloaf recipes call for ground chuck, pork or bacon, eggs, and bread crumbs—all of which add up to a meal low in fiber and high in fat. To rehab this classic, Chef Daniel used lean ground beef and made a sauce with sun-dried tomatoes, tomato puree, and ketchup to add moisture and flavor. Leftovers make a terrific sandwich.

SERVES 6

2 teaspoons olive oil

1 onion, finely chopped

3 garlic cloves, crushed

4 sun-dried tomatoes (without oil), reconstituted in hot water and coarsely chopped

3 tablespoons chopped fresh flat-leaf parsley

¼ cup tomato puree

¼ cup no-salt-added ketchup

1 teaspoon Worcestershire sauce

Nonstick cooking spray

1½ pounds 90% lean ground beef

1 large egg

1 large egg white

¼ teaspoon kosher salt

¼ teaspoon freshly ground black pepper

¾ cup panko (Japanese-style bread crumbs)

Put a skillet over medium heat and coat with the oil. When the oil is hot, add the onion and garlic and cook, stirring, until soft, about 3 minutes. Add the sun-dried tomatoes and continue to cook and stir until well incorporated and completely soft. Stir in the parsley, tomato puree, ketchup, and Worcestershire. Simmer the relish for 5 minutes to bring all the flavors together. Remove from the heat and set aside.

Preheat the oven to 375°F. Coat a 9-by-5-inch loaf pan with nonstick spray.

In a large mixing bowl, combine the ground beef with the tomato relish, egg, and egg white; season with salt and pepper. Sprinkle in the bread crumbs and mix thoroughly with your hands, taking care not to overmix.

Fill the loaf pan with the meat mixture and tap the pan on the counter so it settles. Flatten the top with a spatula. Put the loaf pan on a cookie sheet; this prevents the liquid from dripping and burning on the bottom of the oven.

Bake for 50 minutes or until the meatloaf pulls away from the sides of the pan. Remove the meatloaf from the oven and let rest for about 5 minutes before slicing.

Per serving: 299 calories, 14 g total fat (5 g saturated), 105 mg cholesterol, 330 mg sodium, 26 g protein, 1 g fiber, 15 g carb

Prosciutto-Stuffed Pork Tenderloin with Smoky Tomatoes

Recipe by Chef Jaden Hair

Chef Jaden had the formidable challenge of rehabbing a family's stuffed pork recipe. Passed down through generations, this dish was a downright celebration of the pig: a pork loin stuffed with chorizo sausage and wrapped in 1 pound of bacon. In this elegant remake, Chef Jaden used pork tenderloin—which is leaner than pork loin—and stuffed it with just a few slices of prosciutto. By quickly searing the meat on the stovetop before roasting it in the oven, she locks in the moisture of the lean pork and creates a crisp exterior—no bacon needed!

SERVES 4

PROSCIUTTO-STUFFED PORK:

Nonstick cooking spray

1 (1-pound) pork tenderloin, rinsed and patted dry

¼ teaspoon freshly ground black pepper

2 tablespoons tomato paste

4 thin slices prosciutto

SAUCE:

6 plum (Roma) tomatoes

1 tablespoon extra-virgin olive oil

Juice of ¼ lemon

3 tablespoons chopped fresh basil

1 garlic clove, minced

½ teaspoon smoked paprika

½ teaspoon freshly ground black pepper

Preheat the oven to 350°F. Coat a grill pan or cast-iron skillet with nonstick cooking spray and place over medium-high heat.

Make a 1-inch-deep incision down the length of the tenderloin; do not cut all the way through. Open the meat like a book so that the tenderloin lies flat. Season with pepper. Spread the tomato paste over the pork with the back of a spoon and arrange the prosciutto in one layer over the top. Roll the pork back into a cylinder shape, encasing the stuffing. Using butcher's twine, wrap the stuffed tenderloin evenly, securing the stuffing.

Put the stuffed pork in the hot pan and cook until the meat is browned on all sides, turning with tongs, about 6 to 8 minutes. Transfer the tenderloin to a baking pan, put the tomatoes around it, and place in the oven. Roast until the tomatoes soften and char, about 15 minutes. Remove the roasted tomatoes to a mixing bowl. Continue to roast the tenderloin for an additional 8 to 10 minutes, or until the thickest part of the pork reaches 145°F.

Using a fork, mash the grilled tomatoes into a chunky sauce. Add the oil, lemon juice, basil, garlic, paprika, and pepper. Mix thoroughly and set aside.

To serve, cut the kitchen twine from the pork and discard. Slice the tenderloins into ¼-inch slices. Divide among dinner plates and spoon the smoky tomatoes on top. Serve immediately.

Per serving: 226 calories, 9 g total fat (2 g saturated), 85 mg cholesterol, 500 mg sodium, 29 g protein, 2 g fiber, 7 g carb

Tofu Thai Curry

Recipe by Chef Jet Tila

Coming from a Thai background, Chef Jet knows a thing or two about making an authentic curry. For this lightened-up dish he made the simple swap to light coconut milk to slash fat and calories, and sautéed the tofu instead of deep-frying it. The result is a delicious dish that showcases authentic Thai flavors. "Hot, sour, salty, and sweet are the fundamental flavors of Thai cuisine," says Chef Jet. "This is a perfectly balanced dish."

SERVES 6

2 (15-ounce) cans light coconut milk

¼ cup green curry paste

Peel of 1 lime cut into thin strips

1 onion, thinly sliced

¼ teaspoon red pepper flakes

5 sprigs fresh basil, preferably Thai

1½ pounds firm tofu, patted dry and cut into thin strips

1 cup canned bamboo shoots, drained and rinsed

½ red bell pepper, cored and thinly sliced

1 tablespoon tamarind paste

1 teaspoon light soy sauce

1 teaspoon sugar

1 cup low-sodium vegetable broth, if needed

3 cups cooked basmati rice, for serving

Put a pot over medium heat and add ¼ cup of the coconut milk. Stir in the curry paste and lime peel. Stir-fry for about 1 minute, until the paste starts to thicken. (If the curry starts to sputter, add a small amount of coconut milk.) Cook until it has the consistency of peanut butter.

Stir in the onion, red pepper flakes, basil, and remaining coconut milk. Increase the heat to high and bring the curry to a full boil. Allow to boil for about 10 to 15 minutes or until the sauce reduces and is thick enough to coat the back of a spoon.

Reduce the heat to medium. Add the tofu, bamboo shoots, bell pepper, tamarind, soy sauce, and sugar. Let simmer for about 10 minutes, stirring occasionally. If the sauce becomes too thick, add more broth.

Spoon ½ cup of rice into 6 bowls. Top with the curry and serve immediately.

Per serving: 449 calories, 25 g total fat (15.5 g saturated), 0 mg cholesterol, 496 mg sodium, 17 g protein, 2 g fiber, 41 g carb

Chef Tip: Tamarind

Tamarind is a firm, sticky, and sour-tasting fruit that grows in large brown pods on the tamarind tree, which can be found in Asia and Latin America. In Thai cooking, tamarind paste or pulp is used in a variety of dishes, from famous pad Thai noodles to curries and fish dishes. Tamarind is sold in jars or bottles and is available at specialty food stores and ethnic markets.

Big Island Teriyaki Burger with Grilled Pineapple

Recipe by Chef Govind Armstrong

When Chef Govind went head-to-head with Chef Scott to rehab a family's blue-cheese-and-bacon burger recipe, he didn't bat an eye. As the owner of 8 oz. Burger Bar, with multiple locations all over the country, Chef Govind is a man who knows his burgers. To build a better burger, he started with ground sirloin, a cut that is much leaner than chuck, swapped out thick-cut bacon for Canadian bacon, and reduced the amount of blue cheese—and, in total, trimmed more than 900 calories from the original recipe. For a distinctive Hawaiian twist, he whipped up a homemade teriyaki sauce with grilled pineapple, scallions, ginger, honey, and sesame oil—a combination that really makes this burger unforgettable.

SERVES 4

GRILLED PINEAPPLE TERIYAKI:

Nonstick cooking spray

½ peeled and cored pineapple, cut into wedges

4 scallions

2 cups baby spinach leaves, finely chopped

½ teaspoon grated garlic

½ teaspoon peeled and grated fresh ginger

1 tablespoon reduced-sodium soy sauce

2 tablespoons unseasoned rice vinegar

2 teaspoons honey

⅛ teaspoon sesame oil

BURGERS:

1 pound 95% lean ground sirloin

1 (2-ounce) link lean sweet Italian turkey sausage, such as Jennie-O® Lean Hot Italian Turkey Sausage, casings removed

1 teaspoon granulated onion

1 teaspoon dried oregano

¼ teaspoon ground cloves

¼ teaspoon allspice

½ teaspoon red pepper flakes

Nonstick cooking spray

2 slices Canadian-style bacon, halved

4 Hawaiian sweet or whole wheat hamburger buns, halved and toasted

2 tablespoons crumbled blue cheese

To make the grilled pineapple teriyaki, coat a grill pan with nonstick spray and place over medium-high heat or preheat a gas or charcoal grill and get it very hot. Put the pineapple wedges on the hot grill and cook until the fruit is charred on all sides, turning with tongs, about 10 minutes total. Remove the pineapple from the grill, chop into small pieces, and put into a mixing bowl.

Next, lay the scallions on the hot grill and char on both sides until softened slightly, about 2 minutes. Remove the scallions from the grill, chop, and add to the pineapple. Keep the grill hot; you'll need it to cook the burgers.

To the pineapple mixture, add the spinach, garlic, ginger, soy sauce, vinegar, honey, and sesame oil. Toss well to evenly distribute the ingredients. Set aside to let the flavors meld.

To make the burgers, in a large mixing bowl combine the beef and the turkey sausage. Add the onion powder, oregano, cloves, allspice, and red pepper flakes. Mix gently by hand to combine, being careful not to overwork the meat. Gently form the meat mixture into four burgers. Spray the grill pan or grill with another coating of nonstick spray. Grill the burgers for 4 minutes per side for medium doneness. The burgers should turn easily without sticking. Remove the burgers to a clean side plate and hold warm.

Arrange the Canadian bacon slices on the grill and cook for 1 minute on each side, until they are scored with grill marks.

To assemble the burgers, lay the hamburger patty on the bottom bun and top with bacon and about ¼ cup of the pineapple teriyaki. Finish with a sprinkle of blue cheese and top with the other half of the bun.

Per serving: 382 calories, 11 g total fat (3 g saturated), 81 mg cholesterol, 706 mg sodium, 34 g protein, 3 g fiber, 40 g carb

Beef Burgundy Stew

This version of the classic French beef stew, slow-cooked with chunks of beef, carrots, pearl onions, and mushrooms and simmered in a rich red wine sauce, is proof that you can eat hearty *and* healthy. This comforting winter stew is easy to make and creates an intoxicating aroma that will warm your family from the inside out.

SERVES 8

1 teaspoon canola oil

4 strips turkey bacon

2 pounds lean beef tenderloin, excess fat trimmed, cut into cubes

¼ teaspoon kosher salt

½ teaspoon freshly ground black pepper

3 tablespoons all-purpose flour

2 tablespoons tomato paste

2 cups dry red wine, such as Burgundy

1 quart low-sodium beef broth

3 sprigs fresh thyme

2 sprigs fresh rosemary

Pinch of sugar

4 garlic cloves, chopped

2 cups peeled pearl onions, frozen and thawed

2 carrots, cut into chunks

1 pound assorted wild mushrooms, such as cremini, shiitake, and oyster, stemmed, wiped clean, and quartered

¼ cup fresh flat-leaf parsley, chopped

Place a large Dutch oven over medium heat and coat with the oil. When the oil is hot, add the bacon. Fry until crisp, 3 to 4 minutes. Remove the bacon to a paper-towel-lined plate, crumble, and set aside. Return the pot to high heat, keeping any rendered fat in the pot.

Working in batches, add the beef to the pot and brown the cubes well on all sides, about 6 minutes per batch. Season with salt and pepper. Remove the browned beef to a side platter as it becomes done.

Return all the browned beef to the pot, along with any accumulated juices, and sprinkle with the flour, stirring to make sure the pieces are well coated. Stir in the tomato paste and pour in the wine, stirring to scrape up the flavorful bits from the bottom of the pot. Pour in the beef broth and add the thyme, rosemary, and sugar.

Stir everything together and bring to a simmer, uncovered, until the liquid has thickened a bit, about 15 minutes.

Add the garlic, pearl onions, carrots, mushrooms, and reserved crumbled bacon to the pot. Reduce the heat to low, cover, and simmer for 20 minutes, until the vegetables and meat are tender. Discard the thyme and rosemary stems.

Serve the beef stew with whole wheat noodles or brown rice. Garnish with a sprinkle of chopped parsley.

Per serving: 331 calories, 10 g total fat (3 g saturated), 79 mg cholesterol, 281 mg sodium, 32 g protein, 1 g fiber, 17 g carb

Horseradish Turkey Burgers with Pickled Onions and Jalapeño Mayo

Recipe by Chef Scott Leibfried

Chef Scott went a different route when it came to overhauling an unhealthy burger recipe: he swapped out the beef for ground turkey. Sometimes turkey burgers get a bad rap for being dry or bland, but not in Chef Scott's rendition, which incorporates turkey sausage and bread crumbs. The result? Melt-in-your-mouth, juicy burgers that are considerably leaner than beef—in fact, this rehab slashed the fat in the original recipe by a whopping 85 percent. Chef Scott also pickled his own red onions—a technique that hardly takes any time and is well worth the effort.

SERVES 4

PICKLED ONIONS:

1 cup red wine vinegar

1 tablespoon agave nectar

1 bay leaf

1 fresh thyme sprig

1 teaspoon peppercorns

1 large red onion, halved lengthwise and thinly sliced

JALAPEÑO MAYO:

Nonstick cooking spray

2 jalapeños, stemmed, halved lengthwise, and seeded

2 tablespoons fat-free vegetarian mayonnaise, such as Nayonaise

1 teaspoon Dijon mustard

BURGERS:

½ cup whole wheat panko (Japanese-style bread crumbs)

½ cup skim milk

1 pound lean ground turkey, such as Jennie-O® Lean Ground Turkey

2 (2-ounce) links sweet Italian turkey sausage, such as

Jennie-O® Lean Sweet Italian Turkey Sausage, casings removed

2 scallions, white and green parts, chopped

2 tablespoons jarred grated horseradish, drained

1 tablespoon Dijon mustard

Nonstick cooking spray

4 whole grain hamburger buns, halved and toasted

¼ cup crumbled light blue cheese

4 pieces iceberg lettuce

To make the pickled onions, combine the vinegar, agave nectar, bay leaf, thyme, and peppercorns in a medium pot. Slowly bring to a simmer over medium heat, stirring occasionally to dissolve the agave. Put the onions in a heatproof container, pour the hot vinegar over the top. The onions should be completely submerged in the liquid; put a small plate on top to weigh them down if necessary. Cover and cool to room temperature. Allow the onions to pickle for at least 15 minutes, or up to overnight (the longer, the better).

To make the jalapeño mayo, coat a grill pan with nonstick cooking spray and place over medium-high heat or preheat a gas or charcoal grill and get it very hot. Put the jalapeños, cut side down, on the hot grill and cook until the chiles are charred on all sides, turning with tongs, about 5 minutes total. Remove the jalapeños from the grill (keeping it hot for the burgers); coarsely chop and put into a blender or food processor. Add the mayonnaise substitute and mustard. Blend until smooth. Set aside.

To make the burgers, in a small bowl soak the bread crumbs in the milk and set aside for 5 minutes to allow them to absorb the liquid.

In a large mixing bowl, combine the ground turkey and turkey sausage. Add the wet bread crumbs, scallions, horseradish, and mustard. Mix gently by hand to combine, being careful not to overwork the meat. Gently hand-form the meat mixture into four burgers.

Spray the grill pan or grill with another coating of nonstick spray and make sure it is still hot. Grill the burgers for 5 minutes per side, or until no longer pink in the middle and juices run clear. The burgers should turn easily without sticking. Remove them to a clean side plate so you have enough room to toast the buns. Toast the hamburger buns, cut side down, for 1 minute.

To assemble, smear 1 tablespoon of the jalapeño mayo on the bottom half of each bun. Set the burger on top, followed by the cheese and the pickled onions. Lay a lettuce leaf on top and enclose with the other half of the bun.

Per serving: 461 calories, 15 g total fat (4.5 g saturated), 101 mg cholesterol, 800 mg sodium, 36 g protein, 6 g fiber, 44 g carb

Moroccan Butternut Squash and Chickpea Tagine

A tagine is a ceramic or clay vessel used to slow-cook stews and other dishes. But the word *tagine* also refers to the delicious dish produced by it, which can also be made easily in a regular pot. This Moroccan vegetarian stew is bursting with chickpeas, butternut squash, and signature spices of cinnamon, ginger, and cumin. The sweet-salty combination of apricots, olives, and almonds makes this one-pot dish feel a little exotic.

SERVES 6

1 tablespoon olive oil

1 large onion, chopped

3 garlic cloves, minced

2 teaspoons ground cinnamon

2 teaspoons ground ginger

1 teaspoon ground cumin

1 teaspoon turmeric

¼ teaspoon cayenne

2 carrots, cut into small chunks

1 (2-pound) butternut squash, peeled, halved, seeded, and cut into small chunks (about 4 cups)

1 (15-ounce) can organic diced tomatoes

1 quart water or low-sodium vegetable broth

1 cup couscous

1 (15-ounce) can chickpeas (garbanzo beans), drained and rinsed

8 dried apricots, sliced

½ cup pitted small green olives

¼ cup slivered almonds, toasted

Juice of 1 lemon, plus peel, cut into thick strips

¼ cup chopped fresh cilantro leaves

¼ cup chopped fresh mint leaves

½ cup nonfat plain Greek yogurt, for serving, if desired

Put a Dutch oven or a large pot with a lid over medium heat and coat with the oil. When the oil is hot, add the onion. Cook and stir until the onion is soft, about 5 minutes. Stir in the garlic, cinnamon, ginger, cumin, turmeric, and cayenne and cook for 1 minute, until fragrant.

Stir in the carrots, squash, tomatoes with their juice, and water. Bring to a simmer over high heat. Reduce the heat to low, cover, and simmer for 20 to 25 minutes, until the carrots and squash are fork-tender.

Stir in the couscous, chickpeas, apricots, olives, and almonds. Add the lemon juice and peel. Stir everything together, cover, reduce heat to low, and simmer for roughly another 10 minutes, until the couscous is tender.

Garnish with cilantro and mint before serving. Top with a dollop of yogurt, if desired.

Per serving: 367 calories, 7 g total fat (1 g saturated), 0 mg cholesterol, 546 mg sodium, 11 g protein, 10 g fiber, 67 g carb

Turkey Chili with Baked Corn Chips

Recipe by Chef Spike Mendelsohn

Chili is a favorite meal for many families, and it's practically synonymous with "game day" and tailgating in many parts of the country. When Chef Spike rehabbed a family's over-the-top chili recipe, the first thing he did was swap out ground beef for turkey; then he replaced fried tortilla chips with homemade baked chips and eliminated the mountain of cheese and sour cream. Chef Spike is known for using spices to bring out the flavor of ordinary dishes, and this simple one-pot meal is no exception. By seasoning the chili with cumin, garlic, cayenne, and his grand-mother's secret—cinnamon—he creates layers of sweet, savory, rich flavor.

SERVES 6

CHILI:

2 tablespoons vegetable oil

1 medium onion, chopped

1 red bell pepper, halved, seeded, and chopped

1 celery stalk, halved lengthwise and chopped

½ teaspoon coarse salt

¼ teaspoon freshly ground black pepper

2 garlic cloves, minced

2 tablespoons chili powder

½ teaspoon cayenne pepper

½ teaspoon ground cumin

½ teaspoon ground cinnamon

1 tablespoon agave nectar

1 pound ground white-meat turkey, such as Jennie-O® Extra Lean Ground Turkey Breast

½ pound ground dark-meat turkey, such as Jennie-O® Lean Ground Turkey

1 (28-ounce) can organic low-sodium crushed tomatoes

1 (15-ounce) can white beans, drained and rinsed

2 plum (Roma) tomatoes, chopped

½ jalapeño, minced and seeded if desired

1 cup water or low-sodium vegetable broth

Chopped fresh oregano leaves

Chopped fresh flat-leaf parsley

CHIPS:

3 corn tortillas, cut into triangles

Nonstick cooking spray

Juice of 1 lime

1 teaspoon ground cumin

½ teaspoon kosher salt

Put a large Dutch oven or pot over medium-high heat and coat with the oil. When the oil is hot, add the onion, bell pepper, and celery. Cook and stir until the vegetables become translucent and tender, about 5 minutes. Season with salt and pepper.

Add the garlic, chili powder, cayenne, cumin, cinnamon, and agave nectar. Cook and stir to incorporate the spices, taking care not to burn them. Add the white and dark ground turkey, breaking the meat up with the back of a wooden spoon. Cook and stir until the turkey is no longer pink, about 5 to 7 minutes.

Pour in the canned tomatoes, along with the liquid, and bring to a simmer. Cook for 5 minutes, until slightly thickened. Reduce the heat to medium. Add the beans, fresh tomatoes, and jalapeño. Pour in the water and stir everything together. Gently simmer, uncovered, until the chili is thick, about 30 minutes.

To make the corn chips, preheat the oven to 350°F. Arrange the tortilla wedges in a single layer in a baking pan. Spray the tops with nonstick cooking spray. Drizzle with the lime and sprinkle with cumin and salt. Bake until crisp, about 7 minutes.

To serve, spoon into bowls and top each serving with chopped oregano and parsley. Serve with the baked tortilla chips.

Per serving: 332 calories, 10 g total fat (2 g saturated), 56 mg cholesterol, 702 mg sodium, 34 g protein, 8 g fiber, 32 g carb

Lighter Seafood Gumbo

Recipe by Chef Aida Mollenkamp

Authentic Cajun gumbo is a Louisiana tradition. As far as recipes go, traditional gumbo can have nearly 900 calories per serving and 2,500 milligrams of sodium. Chef Aida showed one family how to keep the tradition alive without compromising their health. The essential ingredients for a real Cajun gumbo are andouille sausage, celery, carrot, onion, and bell peppers—and, of course, it's not real gumbo without okra. Okra has natural thickening properties that are imperative for creating the consistency of the gumbo—so don't leave it out!

SERVES 8

- ½ cup whole wheat flour (see tip, page 17)
- 1 tablespoon vegetable oil
- 8 ounces smoked andouille sausage, sliced
- 1 onion, chopped
- 2 celery stalks, ends trimmed and chopped
- 1 green bell pepper, halved, stemmed, cored, and chopped
- 1 red bell pepper, halved, stemmed, cored, and chopped

- 4 garlic cloves, minced
- 1 tablespoon fresh thyme leaves, chopped
- 1 tablespoon Cajun seasoning, salt-free, such as Frontier
- 2 bay leaves
- 2 cups low-sodium chicken broth
- 1 quart water
- 1 (15-ounce) can low-sodium diced tomatoes
- 8 ounces frozen sliced okra, thawed

- ¾ pound medium peeled and deveined shrimp, tails on (about 15–18)
- 16 ounces lump crabmeat, fresh or canned, drained and picked over for shells
- 2 cups cooked brown rice, for serving
- 2 scallions, white and green parts, thinly sliced, for garnish
- ¼ cup chopped fresh flat-leaf parsley, for garnish

Put a small skillet over medium heat, add the flour, and cook, stirring constantly with a wooden spoon until toasted, about 10 minutes. Take care not to let the flour darken too quickly and burn. Spread the toasted flour on a plate and set aside.

Put a pot or Dutch oven over medium heat and add half of the oil. When the oil is hot, add the sausage and cook until browned on all sides, about 5 minutes. Remove the browned sausage to a side plate and return the pot to medium heat.

To the drippings in the pot, add the remaining oil. When the oil is hot, stir in the onion, celery, bell peppers, and garlic. Stir in the thyme, Cajun seasoning, and bay leaves. Cook, stirring, until the vegetables are soft and fragrant, about 8 minutes.

Sprinkle in the reserved toasted flour, stirring with a wooden spoon until dissolved, with no visible lumps. Once the flour is fully incorporated, slowly pour in the broth, water, and tomatoes (with juices). Bring the mixture to a boil, then stir in the reserved browned sausage; reduce the heat to medium-low. Simmer, stirring occasionally, until the stew is slightly thickened and the flavors have melded, about 30 minutes.

Add the thawed okra and cook until the okra is heated through and the sauce is slightly more thickened, about 5 minutes; if it becomes too thick, add more water. Stir in the shrimp and crab, cover the pot, and simmer gently until the shrimp is pink and cooked through, about 5 to 7 minutes. Taste the gumbo to check the seasoning.

Serve gumbo in bowls over cooked rice, garnished with scallions and parsley.

Per serving: 293 calories, 8 g total fat (2 g saturated), 110 mg cholesterol, 757 mg sodium, 28 g protein, 5 g fiber, 29 g carb

Chef Tip: Roux

Great-tasting gumbo begins with a roux, a thickening paste typically made by combining flour with the same amount of butter or oil. In order to eliminate extra fat and calories, try making Chef Aida's "dry roux," a technique that slashes the fat and calories by skipping the butter or oil and simply browning the flour in a dry skillet until toasted to a deep nutty brown. Dry roux adds a rich flavor and viscosity not only to gumbo but also to soups, sauces, and stews.

Turkey Pot Pie

This lightened-up pot pie made with turkey breast and fresh vegetables is so good, you won't miss the heavy, cream-based sauce commonly found in this dish. Traditional puff-pastry crusts also contribute fat and calories, so instead, a slimmed-down quick biscuit crust does the trick. Feel free to use whatever vegetables you have on hand, as this is an ideal dish for using up leftovers!

SERVES 4

POT PIE:

1¼ pounds boneless, skinless turkey breast

1 quart low-sodium chicken broth

1 tablespoon canola oil

2 carrots, finely chopped

2 celery stalks, finely chopped

1 small onion, finely chopped

½ teaspoon freshly ground black pepper

½ pound green beans, ends trimmed and chopped

2 garlic cloves, minced

3 tablespoons all-purpose flour

1 cup frozen peas, run under cool water to thaw

2 tablespoons chopped fresh flat-leaf parsley

1 tablespoon fresh thyme leaves

2 teaspoons fresh rosemary leaves, finely chopped

BISCUIT TOPPING:

1 cup all-purpose flour

1 teaspoon baking powder

½ teaspoon baking soda

¼ teaspoon salt

½ cup low-fat buttermilk

2 tablespoons light butter, such as Land O'Lakes, melted

Put the turkey breast in a pot and cover with the broth. Bring to a simmer over medium-high heat. Simmer, covered, until the turkey is poached and just cooked through, about 35 minutes. Remove the turkey to a cutting board to cool and reserve the broth. When cool enough to handle, cut the turkey meat into cubes and set aside.

Coat a deep skillet with the oil and put over medium heat. When the oil is hot, add the carrots, celery, and onion; season with pepper. Cook and stir until the vegetables are tender, about 5 minutes. Add the green beans and garlic; continue to cook and stir for 3 to 4 minutes, until the green beans begin to soften. Sprinkle the vegetables with the flour and cook, stirring, until the flour dissolves into a paste.

Gradually whisk in the reserved broth, stirring to prevent lumps. Simmer and whisk for 10 minutes, until the sauce starts to thicken; it should look like cream-of-chicken soup.

Mix in the reserved turkey, peas, parsley, thyme, and rosemary. Simmer for 1 or 2 minutes, stirring now and then, until all the ingredients are well combined. Remove from the heat and cover to hold warm.

To make the biscuit topping, in a mixing bowl combine the flour, baking powder, baking soda, and salt. Add the buttermilk and melted butter and mix gently, just until the dry ingredients are moistened.

Preheat the oven to 400°F.

To assemble, pour the turkey-and-vegetable mixture into a 13-by-9-inch baking dish. Spoon the biscuit dough over the top in small, dumpling-size balls. Bake for 25 to 30 minutes, until the biscuits are golden. Spoon into bowls and serve immediately.

Allow the casserole to rest for a few minutes. When the mixture is no longer bubbling, spoon into bowls and serve immediately.

Per serving: 476 calories, 11 g total fat (4 g saturated), 102 mg cholesterol, 700 mg sodium, 47 g protein, 6 g fiber, 48 g carb

REHAB TIP: LOW-FAT BUTTERMILK Low-fat buttermilk is thicker and creamier than skim or low-fat milk, and even contains probiotics (beneficial bacteria that help keep your digestive system healthy). It's a great substitute for heavy cream or full-fat buttermilk, especially in breakfast breads such as biscuits, pancakes, and coffee cake. You can also make a simple and delicious salad dressing with low-fat buttermilk, fat-free sour cream, and any fresh herbs you prefer.

Chicken-Fried Steak with Mashed Potatoes

Recipe by Chef Jet Tila

Chicken-fried steak gets its name from following its Southern cousin, fried chicken. Battered and fried to a crisp, the meat is then doused in gravy and served with buttery mashed potatoes. When Chef Jet approached the rehab for this recipe, he cut back on the amount of meat needed by pounding the beef to a thinner cut with a mallet. By extending the meat in this way, you get a serving size that seems bigger than it actually is—and you save on calories and fat. Instead of dipping the meat in a rich batter and deep-frying, he dusted it with whole wheat flour and cornmeal to get a nice crispy coating and then pan-fried it. Just a tablespoon of fat-free sour cream is all that's needed to add fluffy richness to the mashed potatoes.

SERVES 4

STEAK:

Nonstick cooking spray

¼ cup all-purpose white flour

1 cup liquid egg substitute, such as Egg Beaters

¼ cup yellow cornmeal

¼ cup whole wheat flour

2 tablespoons cornstarch

1 teaspoon paprika

1 pound round steak, boneless, cut into 4 portions

¼ teaspoon kosher salt

½ teaspoon freshly ground black pepper

1 tablespoon canola oil

1 (15-ounce) can low-sodium beef broth

1 tablespoon water

¼ cup low-fat milk

MASHED POTATOES:

1½ pounds russet potatoes, scrubbed and cut into large chunks

¼ cup low-sodium chicken broth, heated

1 tablespoon fat-free sour cream

Salt and pepper to taste

Preheat the oven to 350°F. Coat a baking pan with nonstick spray and set aside.

Create a breading station. Spread the all-purpose flour on a large plate. Pour the egg substitute into a wide, shallow bowl and whisk with a fork. On a separate plate, combine the cornmeal, whole wheat flour, 1 tablespoon of the cornstarch, and paprika. Mix together with a fork.

Using a meat mallet or the bottom of a heavy pan, pound the steak until ¼ inch thick. Season both sides of the steaks with salt and pepper. Working with one at a time, dredge the steak in the flour, shaking off the excess; dip in the egg substitute; then dredge in the cornmeal mixture to coat both sides. Set the breaded steak on a side platter.

Put a large nonstick skillet over medium heat and coat with 1½ teaspoons of the oil. When the oil is hot, add two pieces of the steak; cook until browned on both sides, turning once, 3 to 5 minutes total. Remove the steak from the skillet and set in the prepared baking pan. Repeat with the remaining 1½ teaspoons of oil and two pieces of steak. Remove the last two pieces of steak to the baking pan, keeping the skillet on the stove. Transfer the baking pan with the steaks to the oven and bake until cooked through, about 10 minutes.

To make the gravy, add the broth to the skillet drippings and simmer over medium-high heat, stirring occasionally, until reduced to about 1 cup, 3 to 5 minutes.

In a small bowl, whisk the water and the remaining 1 tablespoon of cornstarch until smooth. Stir the cornstarch mixture into the skillet gravy and cook until thickened, 1 to 2 minutes. Stir in the milk. Cover and keep warm.

To make the mashed potatoes, put the potatoes in a large pot and cover with cold salted water. Bring to a boil over high heat. Reduce heat to low and simmer, partially covered, until tender, 10 to 15 minutes.

Drain the potatoes and return to the pot (with the heat off). Using a potato masher or handheld mixer, mash the potatoes, adding enough hot broth to make a chunky puree. Stir in the sour cream and season with salt and pepper.

To serve, divide the steak among four plates and add a spoonful of mashed potatoes on the side. Top steak and potatoes with a ladleful of gravy.

Per serving: 523 calories, 14 g total fat (4 g saturated), 79 mg cholesterol, 431 mg sodium, 41 g protein, 4 g fiber, 57 g carb

Green Bean Casserole

Recipe by Chef Laura Vitale

This iconic dish of the 1950s still has a place on many families' holiday dinner tables. But don't let the green beans fool you—there's nothing wholesome about this creamy casserole. Chef Laura reinvents it for the 21st century by using fresh mushrooms and a little reduced-fat cream cheese in place of canned soup. Topped with crunchy french-fried onions, her recipe will take the place of the old casserole on your dinner table for generations to come.

SERVES 8

Nonstick cooking spray

1½ pounds green beans, trimmed and washed

1 tablespoon olive oil

2 slices bacon, chopped

1 small onion, diced

1 (10-ounce) package cremini mushrooms, wiped clean and thinly sliced

2 garlic cloves, minced

½ teaspoon kosher salt

¼ teaspoon freshly ground black pepper

2 tablespoons all-purpose flour

1 cup vegetable broth

½ cup nonfat milk

2 tablespoons reduced-fat onion-and-chive-flavored cream cheese, at room temperature

¼ cup freshly grated Parmesan cheese

1 cup canned french-fried onions

Preheat the oven to 400°F. Coat a 2-quart baking dish with nonstick spray and set aside. Bring a pot of water to a boil and also have ready a bowl filled with water and ice.

Cut the green beans into bite-size pieces and add to the boiling water for about 5 minutes; immediately drain, then shock them in the ice water to stop the cooking process. Once the green beans are completely cool, put them into a large mixing bowl. Set aside.

Put a wide skillet with high sides over medium heat and coat with the oil. When the oil is hot, add the bacon and cook until it begins to crisp, about 3 minutes. Add the onion and cook, stirring, until it softens and begins to brown. Add the mushrooms, garlic, salt, and pepper. Cook, stirring, until the mushrooms lose their moisture, about 15 to 20 minutes.

Sprinkle in the flour and stir to incorporate. Pour in the broth and milk; bring to a boil and cook until slightly thickened, about 5 minutes. Stir in the cream cheese and Parmesan.

Pour the sauce into the bowl of green beans and mix to combine. Pour the green bean mixture into the prepared baking dish and top with the french-fried onions. Bake for about 12 to 15 minutes or until the top is golden brown.

 To watch a how-to video for this recipe, check out www.RecipeRehab.com.

Per serving: 139 calories, 8 g total fat (2 g saturated), 8 mg cholesterol, 370 mg sodium, 6 g protein, 4 g fiber, 14 g carb

Pumpkin Bars with Cream Cheese Frosting, page 149

Part 7

CLASSIC
DESSERTS

Nearly No-Fat Brownies with Peanut Butter Sauce and Caramelized Bananas

Recipe by Chef Scott Leibfried

Truth be told, rehabbing a brownie didn't present that great a challenge for Chef Scott. So he upped the ante by creating a truly refined plated dessert with homemade peanut butter sauce and caramelized bananas. Chef Scott slashed fat and calories by using unsweetened cocoa powder to impart deep chocolate flavor and nonfat yogurt to keep the brownies moist. The sweetness of the caramelized bananas combined with the rich peanut butter and fudgy chocolate make this a true standout dessert.

MAKES 16 BROWNIES

BROWNIES:

Nonstick cooking spray

½ cup oat flour

½ cup unsweetened cocoa powder

½ teaspoon baking soda

1 cup nonfat vanilla yogurt

¼ cup egg substitute, such as Egg Beaters

½ cup sugar

SAUCE:

1 (12-ounce) can fat-free evaporated milk, such as Carnation

¼ cup creamy no-salted-added organic peanut butter

TOPPING:

1 banana, peeled

1½ teaspoons sugar

To make the brownies, preheat the oven to 350°F. Coat an 8-by-8-inch baking dish with nonstick spray and set aside.

Sift the flour, cocoa powder, and baking soda into a mixing bowl. Add the yogurt, egg substitute, and sugar. Mix well, until the batter is smooth. Pour the batter into the prepared baking dish, smoothing the top evenly with a spatula.

Bake for 20 to 25 minutes, until a wooden toothpick inserted into the center of the brownies comes out with a bit of chocolate clinging to it. Cool in the baking dish before cutting.

To make the sauce, in a small pot combine the evaporated milk and peanut butter over medium-low heat. Gently simmer, stirring occasionally, until the peanut butter is incorporated and the milk is slightly thickened, about 10 minutes.

To caramelize the banana, cut into slightly angled slices and sprinkle with the sugar. Hold a kitchen torch 2 inches above the surface of the bananas, or broil them in the oven for 3 minutes, until golden brown.

To serve, pool some peanut butter sauce on the bottom of a dessert plate, set a brownie in the center, and top with caramelized bananas.

REHAB TIP: EVAPORATED MILK Canned evaporated milk is not the same thing as sweetened condensed milk, which contains a lot of added sugar. Evaporated milk contains about half of the water of regular milk, with no added sugar. Because the water is evaporated, the resulting milk product is thick and creamy. Fat-free evaporated milk is a great choice for healthy baking.

Per serving (2 brownies): 215 calories, 6 g total fat (1 g saturated), 0 mg cholesterol, 163 mg sodium, 9 g protein, 3 g fiber, 36 g carb

Sour Cream Coffee Cake

Perfect for the afternoon kaffeeklatsch at work or for a leisurely Sunday brunch, this coffee cake has an irresistible taste and a timeless aesthetic. And unlike those heavy bricks of cake at your local coffee shop, a serving clocks in at fewer than 300 calories and just 6 grams of fat. Fat-free sour cream, applesauce, and a little oil keep the cake moist, while a mixture of white and wheat flours creates a dense, satisfying texture. If you consider yourself a good baker but aren't the best cake decorator, try purchasing a Bundt pan with a fun design—it can turn a simple cake into a special-occasion dessert.

SERVES 12

CAKE:

Nonstick cooking spray

½ cup chopped walnuts

2 cups all-purpose flour

1 cup whole wheat flour

1 teaspoon baking soda

1 teaspoon salt

1½ teaspoons ground cinnamon

½ teaspoon ground allspice

1½ cups nonfat sour cream

¾ cup unsweetened applesauce

2 tablespoons canola oil

½ cup sugar

1 teaspoon vanilla extract

2 large egg whites

1 large egg

GLAZE:

¾ cup powdered sugar

2 tablespoons 100 percent natural apple juice

Preheat the oven to 350°F. Coat a Bundt pan with cooking spray and sprinkle the walnuts evenly around the pan. Set aside.

In a mixing bowl, sift together the flours, baking soda, salt, cinnamon, and allspice.

In a separate bowl, combine the sour cream, applesauce, oil, sugar, and vanilla. Using a handheld electric mixer, beat on medium speed until well mixed, about 3 minutes. Scrape down the sides of the bowl. Add the egg whites and whole egg, beating well to incorporate.

Reduce the mixer speed to low and gradually add the flour mixture to the sour cream mixture. Beat until the batter is smooth, without any lumps.

Scrape the batter into the prepared pan and smooth the surface with a spatula; the pan should be about halfway full. Tap the pan firmly on the countertop a few times to level and knock out any air bubbles. Bake until the cake is golden and a toothpick comes out clean when inserted into the center, about 45 to 50 minutes. Cool in the pan for 15 minutes. Set a serving plate or platter firmly on top of the Bundt pan and carefully flip it over to invert the cake onto the plate.

To prepare the glaze, in a mixing bowl combine the powdered sugar and apple juice. Stir constantly until the sugar dissolves and the glaze is completely smooth. The glaze should be thick yet pourable; add more apple juice, as necessary, to achieve desired consistency. Pour the glaze over the cake, letting it run down the sides; let dry for about 15 minutes before serving.

Per serving: 263 calories, 6 g total fat (1 g saturated), 16 mg cholesterol, 355 mg sodium, 6 g protein, 2 g fiber, 45 g carb

Mocha Chocolate Cake

Recipe by Chef Jaden Hair

Everyone has a favorite chocolate cake recipe. When Chef Jaden took on the challenge of over-hauling one family's beloved recipe, she had her work cut out for her: Clocking in at 1,055 calories and 62 grams of fat per serving, this was one recipe in desperate need of a rehab. To cut back on the fat, she used fat-free sour cream, reduced-fat cream cheese, and light butter to add moisture to the cake. She also reduced the calories by getting rid of the white sugar in the batter and the powdered sugar in the frosting. In the end, she saved more than 650 calories and 50 grams of fat by making healthy substitutions. This pretty frosted layer cake has a hint of coffee flavor that makes it distinctive and rich—a true "grown-up" dessert.

SERVES 8

Baking spray (cooking spray with flour)

BATTER:

⅓ cup light butter, such as Land O'Lakes, at room temperature

¾ cup nonfat sour cream

1 cup Truvia Baking Blend

¾ cup liquid egg substitute, such as Egg Beaters

2 teaspoons pure vanilla extract

½ cup unsweetened cocoa powder

1 teaspoon baking soda

¼ teaspoon salt

¾ cup brewed strong coffee, hot

2 cups whole wheat pastry flour

FROSTING:

1 cup Truvia Baking Blend

1 teaspoon cornstarch

4 ounces reduced-fat cream cheese, at room temperature

2 tablespoons light butter, such as Land O'Lakes, at room temperature

3 tablespoons nonfat milk

1 teaspoon pure vanilla extract

⅓ cup unsweetened cocoa powder

Pinch salt

Heat the oven to 350°F. Coat the bottoms of two 9-inch round cake pans with baking spray. Set aside.

In a large mixing bowl, combine the butter and sour cream. Using a handheld electric mixer, beat on medium speed until light and fluffy, about 3 minutes. Scrape down the sides of the bowl. Add the Truvia, egg substitute, vanilla, cocoa powder, baking soda, and salt. Continue to beat until the mixture is well blended, about 3 minutes.

Pour in the hot coffee and beat for another 2 minutes. Reduce the mixer speed to low and gradually add the flour. Mix until combined, with no visible lumps.

Divide the batter between the cake pans, smoothing the surface with a spatula. Bake for 30 to 35 minutes, until the cakes are springy and fairly firm to the touch. Cool in the pans for about 10 minutes. Loosen each cake from the sides of the pan by running a thin metal spatula around the edges. Turn the cakes out onto a wire rack to cool completely.

To prepare the frosting, combine the Truvia and cornstarch in a food processor; pulse until the mixture is very fine and resembles powdered sugar. The finer the mixture, the better the frosting will turn out.

In a mixing bowl, combine the cream cheese, butter, milk, and vanilla. Using a handheld electric mixer, beat on medium speed until the cream cheese mixture is well blended and smooth. Reduce the mixer speed to low and sprinkle in the cocoa powder, salt, and pulsed sugar. Continue to beat until the frosting is well blended and smooth, about 1 minute.

With a metal spatula, spread about ½ cup of the frosting on top of one of the cooled cake rounds. Carefully place the other cake on top and frost the top with the remaining frosting.

Per serving: 373 calories, 10 g total fat (5 g saturated), 17 mg cholesterol, 479 mg sodium, 10 g protein, 7 g fiber, 82 g carb

Strawberry Cheesecake

Cheesecake is a delicious but indulgent dessert no matter how you slice it. A traditional cheese-cake recipe gets its richness—as well as its high fat and cholesterol content—from cream cheese and sour cream, as well as several whole eggs. This rehabbed version, inspired by Italian cheesecake, incorporates ricotta cheese, which achieves that creamy decadence we all love while creating a lighter, airier texture. Neufchâtel cheese and Greek yogurt add richness and density, while a crown of ruby red strawberries contributes nutrients and vibrant color.

SERVES 12

Nonstick cooking spray

CRUST:

10 whole low-fat cinnamon graham crackers, broken in half

¼ teaspoon ground cinnamon

2 tablespoons light butter, such as Land O'Lakes, melted

2 tablespoons water

FILLING:

1 (8-ounce) package Neufchâtel cheese, at room temperature

1 (15-ounce) container part-skim ricotta cheese

¾ cup sugar

2 large eggs

3 large egg whites

3 tablespoons cornstarch

1 teaspoon pure vanilla extract

½ teaspoon salt

Finely grated zest of 1 lemon

½ cup nonfat vanilla Greek yogurt

2 cups frozen and thawed strawberry halves

2 teaspoons sugar

To make the crust, preheat the oven to 325°F. Coat an 8-inch springform pan with nonstick spray. Set aside.

Put the graham crackers and cinnamon in a food processor and pulse until finely ground. Add the melted butter and water and pulse until moistened. Firmly press the crumb mixture over the bottom of the pan, using your fingers or the smooth bottom of a glass. Bake the crust for 10 minutes.

To make the filling, in a large bowl, beat the cream cheese with a handheld electric mixer on low speed for 1 minute, until free of any lumps. Add the ricotta and continue to beat until smooth. Gradually add the sugar and beat until creamy, 1 to 2 minutes. Periodically scrape down the sides of the bowl and the beaters. Add the eggs, one at a time, and continue to beat slowly until combined. Add the egg whites and beat until incorporated. Add the cornstarch and beat until incorporated.

Stop the mixer and, using a rubber spatula, stir in the vanilla, salt, and lemon zest, then blend in the yogurt. Pour the filling into the crust-lined pan and smooth the top with a spatula.

Set the cheesecake pan on a cookie sheet so it will be easier to move in and out of the oven. Bake the cheesecake for 50 minutes; it should still jiggle slightly when you gently shake the pan. (It will firm up after chilling.) Let cool in the pan for 30 minutes. Chill in the refrigerator, loosely covered, for at least 4 hours or up to overnight.

Loosen the cheesecake from the sides of the pan by running a thin metal spatula around the inside rim. Unmold and transfer to a cake plate.

In a bowl, mash the strawberries with the sugar. Top the cheesecake evenly with the strawberries. Slice the cheesecake with a thin, non-serrated knife.

Per serving: 242 calories, 9 g total fat (5 g saturated), 57 mg cholesterol, 268 mg sodium, 9 g protein, 1 g fiber, 32 g carb

REHAB TIP: NEUFCHÂTEL CHEESE   Neufchâtel cheese is a great swap for cream cheese in almost any baking or cooking recipe. Like cream cheese, Neufchâtel cheese is creamy, dense, and spreadable, and has a slightly tangy taste. But Neufchâtel cheese is naturally lower in fat and calories than regular cream cheese, plus it has slightly more moisture—making it a great choice for dips, spreads, and "cream cheese" frosting.

Individual Phyllo Apple Cups

Recipe by Chef Spike Mendelsohn

Apple pie is an all-time American favorite, so when Chef Spike went head-to-head against Chef Mareya to rehab this beloved classic, he knew he had to nail it. The first thing that had to go was the buttery double crust. Having grown up in a Greek household, Chef Spike knows a thing or two about phyllo dough, which are tissue-paper-thin pastry sheets. Phyllo makes a terrific low-fat alternative to heavier doughs like pie crust and puff pastry. Chef Spike also relied on the natural sweetness of the apples and dried cranberries to cut down on the amount of added sweetener. These pretty little "pies" are easy to make and keep portion sizes in check.

SERVES 12

Nonstick cooking spray

2 pounds Granny Smith apples, peeled, cored, and cut into ½-inch chunks

⅓ cup dried cranberries

Juice and finely grated zest of 1 lemon

2 tablespoons agave nectar

2 teaspoons freshly grated ginger

1 teaspoon ground cinnamon

½ teaspoon allspice

3 tablespoons unsalted butter, melted

2 tablespoons water

4 (9-by-14-inch) sheets phyllo pastry, thawed

1 cup fat-free vanilla frozen yogurt

Preheat the oven to 350°F. Coat a standard muffin pan with nonstick spray. Set aside.

In a large pot, combine the apples, cranberries, lemon juice, zest, agave, ginger, cinnamon, and allspice. Cook over medium heat, stirring occasionally, until the juices in the pot thicken and very little syrup remains, about 10 minutes. Set aside to cool.

In a small bowl, mix the melted butter and water. Unfold the phyllo, lay one sheet on a cutting board, and brush the dough with the melted butter-water mixture—be sure to keep the pastry you are not working with covered with a damp towel to prevent it from drying out. Repeat three times, stacking the layers of dough on top of each other so that you have four layers.

Cut the stack of phyllo sheets three times crosswise and then cut again lengthwise twice so you have 12 even squares. Lay the phyllo squares in the wells of the muffin pan and gently press them into the cups, letting the edges fold and overlap naturally.

Spoon ¼ cup of the cooled apple mixture into the phyllo cups. Bake for 12 to 15 minutes or until nicely browned. Let the apple cups cool in the pan before trying to remove them. Serve warm with a small spoonful of frozen yogurt.

 To watch a how-to video for this recipe, check out www.RecipeRehab.com.

Per serving (one Apple Cup): 144 calories, 4 g total fat (3 g saturated), 8 mg cholesterol, 74 mg sodium, 2 g protein, 4 g fiber, 27 g carb

Apple Oatmeal Crumble

Recipe by Chef Mareya Ibrahim

Chef Mareya's answer to the Apple Pie Face-Off also eliminated the buttery crust, but instead of re-creating it, she simply went crustless with this rich, delicious apple crumble that's topped with crunchy graham crackers and heart-healthy oats. For the filling she used Golden Delicious apples, which are a little higher in sugar than other varieties, so she needed to add only a few tablespoons of brown sugar. A warm bowlful of this hearty crumble is sure to satisfy your deepest apple pie cravings.

SERVES 8

CRUST:

⅓ cup rolled oats

8 low-fat graham crackers

1 large egg white

Nonstick cooking spray

FILLING:

1 tablespoon nondairy butter spread, such as Earth Balance

6 cups thinly sliced Golden Delicious apples

⅓ cup raisins

2 tablespoons dark brown sugar, packed

1 teaspoon ground cinnamon

1 teaspoon ground ginger

2 tablespoons freshly squeezed lemon juice

½ teaspoon pure vanilla extract

2 tablespoons cornstarch or arrowroot powder

TOPPING:

½ cup rolled oats

¼ teaspoon ground cinnamon, plus more for dusting

Pinch kosher salt

2 teaspoons nondairy butter spread, such as Earth Balance, cold

8 tablespoons nonfat, no-sugar-added whipped topping, such as 365

To prepare the crust, preheat the oven to 350°F.

In a food processor, pulse the oats and graham crackers until finely ground. Add the egg white and process until blended.

Coat a 9-inch pie dish with nonstick cooking spray and press the crumb mixture evenly into the pie pan to make the crust. Bake for 10 minutes. Set aside, keeping the oven on.

To prepare the filling, in a large skillet over medium heat, melt the butter substitute. Add the apples, raisins, and brown sugar. Cook, stirring, for about 5 minutes. Sprinkle in the cinnamon and ginger, stirring to combine. Remove the pan from the heat. Add the lemon juice, vanilla, and cornstarch, stirring to fully incorporate. Spoon the apple filling into the crust.

To prepare the topping, in a small bowl combine the oats, cinnamon, salt, and butter substitute. Mix with your hands to create a crumb texture. Sprinkle evenly over the filling.

Bake the crumble for about 20 to 25 minutes, until golden brown. Scoop into bowls and top with a dollop of nonfat whipped cream and a dusting of cinnamon, if desired.

Per serving: 165 calories, 3 g total fat (1 g saturated), 0 mg cholesterol, 89 mg sodium, 3 g protein, 4 g fiber, 32 g carb

Pumpkin Bars with Cream Cheese Frosting

Recipe by Chef Laura Vitale

Pumpkin bars are a fall tradition in many households. While pumpkin is actually a great source of vitamins A, K, and E, as well as potassium and magnesium, many pumpkin desserts are made with so much oil and sugar that the nutritional value of the pumpkin is overshadowed. Chef Laura lightened up these bars by using applesauce in place of oil, swapping out sugar for Splenda, and substituting oat flour for white flour. At fewer than 200 calories per serving, you can feel good about making these deliciously moist, spiced bars an annual tradition for your family.

MAKES 16 BARS

BARS:

Nonstick cooking spray

2 cups oat flour or whole wheat pastry flour

1 tablespoon pumpkin pie spice

2 teaspoons baking powder

1 teaspoon baking soda

½ teaspoon salt

1 large egg

3 large egg whites

2 cups canned pumpkin puree

½ cup unsweetened applesauce

½ cup Splenda Brown Sugar Blend

⅓ cup Splenda Sugar Blend

½ cup skim milk

2 teaspoons pure vanilla extract

GLAZE:

4 ounces low-fat cream cheese, at room temperature

1 teaspoon pure vanilla extract

1 tablespoon unsalted butter, at room temperature

1½ cups powdered sugar

Preheat the oven to 350°F. Line a jelly roll pan with parchment paper and coat with nonstick spray. Set aside.

In a large bowl, mix together the dry ingredients: oat flour, pumpkin pie spice, baking powder, baking soda, and salt. Set aside.

In another bowl, whisk together the egg, egg whites, pumpkin, applesauce, both kinds of Splenda, milk, and vanilla. Pour the wet ingredients into the dry and mix everything well to combine. Spread the batter into the prepared jelly roll pan.

Bake for 25 minutes or until a toothpick inserted into the center comes out clean. Allow to cool at room temperature for about 10 minutes, then pop it into the fridge for about 15 minutes or until completely cooled.

To prepare the glaze, in a large bowl, with a whisk or handheld electric mixer, cream together the cream cheese, vanilla, butter, and powdered sugar until fully incorporated and fluffy.

Spread the frosting on the cooled cake and allow it to set for just a few minutes in the fridge. Cut into 16 bars.

Per serving (1 bar): 187 calories, 3 g total fat (1 g saturated), 17 mg cholesterol, 266 mg sodium, 4 g protein, 3 g fiber, 34 g carb

Dairy-Free Decadent Chocolate Cupcakes

Recipe by Chef Laura Vitale

These days it seems as if cupcake shops are popping up on every street corner in America. Not only are those cupcakes pricey, but most of them are topped with a mound of buttercream frosting, making them so sweet and rich that they're a bit overwhelming. These rehabbed chocolate cupcakes couldn't be simpler to make, and both the batter and the topping are dairy-free, so they're great for anyone with a dairy sensitivity or allergy. Store the cupcakes unfrosted in an airtight container.

MAKES 12 CUPCAKES

1½ cups all-purpose flour

½ cup unsweetened cocoa powder

¼ teaspoon salt

½ teaspoon baking soda

½ teaspoon baking powder

½ cup unsweetened applesauce

½ cup sugar

¼ cup light brown sugar, loosely packed

1 teaspoon pure vanilla extract

1 cup plain unsweetened almond milk

1 large egg

12 tablespoons soy whipped topping

Preheat the oven to 350°F. Line a cupcake pan with liners and set side.

In a small bowl, whisk together the flour, cocoa powder, salt, baking soda, and baking powder. Set aside.

In a large bowl, cream together the applesauce, both kinds of sugar, vanilla, almond milk, and egg. Stir in the dry ingredients and mix them through just enough to incorporate them. Do not overmix.

Using a large ice cream scoop, divide the mixture among the liners and bake them for about 20 to 22 minutes. Let the cupcakes cool completely.

Top with soy whipped topping before serving.

Per serving (1 cupcake): 129 calories, 2 g total fat (1 g saturated), 16 mg cholesterol, 144 mg sodium, 3 g protein, 2 g fiber, 27 g carb

Chef Tip: Cocoa Powder

Cocoa powder is made when chocolate liquor is pressed to remove three-quarters of its cocoa butter. The remaining cocoa solids are processed to make fine unsweetened cocoa powder. Natural unsweetened cocoa is low in calories and virtually fat-free; it gives a deep chocolate flavor to a variety of baked goods, like cupcakes, brownies, and cookies. You can also add it to plain icing to make chocolate icing in a snap.

Low-Fat Lemon Trifle with Fresh Raspberries

Recipe by Chef Daniel Green

A native of England, Chef Daniel grew up eating English trifle, a thick custard dessert layered with fruit, whipped cream, and pound cake—a cake that got its name from using one pound each of sugar, butter, and flour! A triumphant trifle is all about showing off the layers and colors in a pretty glass vessel. This rehabbed trifle uses lemon pudding and nonfat milk for the custard and crumbled store-bought meringue cookies to replace the cake. Fresh raspberries add a bit of tartness to balance out the sweet flavors and lend a bright pop of color. This virtually no-fat trifle doesn't even require you to turn on the oven, takes just minutes to assemble, and is a real stunner at a dinner party.

SERVES 4

12 white meringue cookies, crushed

2 cups nonfat plain Greek yogurt

1 (3.4-ounce) box sugar-free instant lemon pudding mix

2 cups nonfat milk, cold

2 pints fresh raspberries

Finely grated zest of 1 lemon

Fresh mint leaves, for garnish (optional)

In a mixing bowl, combine the crushed meringues and yogurt. Fold together until combined. Cover bowl and transfer to the refrigerator.

In a separate bowl, combine the pudding powder with the cold milk. Using a handheld electric mixer, beat on medium-low speed until light and fluffy. Refrigerate until firm, at least 10 minutes.

Put the raspberries in another bowl and mash with a fork until the raspberries are broken down but still a bit chunky.

To build the trifle, use 4 parfait glasses or any other tall, elegant clear glasses you like. Spoon a couple of tablespoons of the meringue-yogurt mixture into the bottom of the glass. Top with a couple of spoonfuls of the lemon pudding and a couple of spoonfuls of the smashed raspberries. Grate the lemon zest on top and garnish with fresh mint, if desired.

Per serving: 351 calories, 1 g total fat (0 g saturated), 3 mg cholesterol, 458 mg sodium, 18 g protein, 8 g fiber, 69 g carb

Gluten-Free Fudgy Beet Brownie Bites

Recipe by Chef Aida Mollenkamp

Gluten-free baking can pose a real challenge for even the most experienced bakers, but Chef Aida didn't bat an eye when she rehabbed these brownies. In addition to swapping out white, all-purpose flour for gluten-free brown rice flour, her other secret weapon was beets, which she added to the batter. The vegetable's natural sugar is a better option than refined white sugar, plus the ruby red color adds a pretty hue to the brownies. You would never know that these moist, chewy brownies get their richness from a vegetable!

MAKES 24 BROWNIES

Nonstick cooking spray

¾ cup unsweetened cocoa powder

¼ cup brown rice flour (or any type of gluten-free flour you prefer)

1 teaspoon baking powder

½ teaspoon fine salt

½ teaspoon ground cinnamon

1 medium red beet, peeled and coarsely chopped

⅔ cup low-fat plain yogurt

⅔ cup unrefined cane sugar

1 large egg

2 large egg whites

1 teaspoon pure vanilla extract

Preheat the oven to 350°F. Coat a 24-well mini-muffin pan with nonstick spray. Set aside.

In a large mixing bowl, whisk together the cocoa powder, rice flour, baking powder, salt, and cinnamon and set aside.

Put the chopped beet in a food processor and pulse until very fine. Measure out ¾ cup and save the rest for another use.

In a mixing bowl, combine the beet, yogurt, sugar, egg, egg whites, and vanilla. Stir briefly until evenly incorporated. Stir in the cocoa powder mixture until just incorporated.

Spoon the batter into the prepared muffin tin and bake until a tester inserted into the center of the brownies comes out clean, 15 to 20 minutes.

Cool the brownies in the pan for 10 minutes before turning out onto a serving platter.

Per serving (2 brownies): 89 calories, 2 g total fat (1 g saturated), 16 mg cholesterol, 169 mg sodium, 3 g protein, 2 g fiber, 18 g carb

Mini Peach and Blueberry Cobbler

Recipe by Chef Govind Armstrong

For this cobbler rehab, Chef Govind faced a formidable challenge: the original recipe was created by a family of champion barbecue pit masters who used two sticks of butter plus a little rendered pork fat for that authentic "country" flavor. Chef Govind lightened up the topping with rolled oats, flaxseed, and almond flour; nixed syrupy canned peaches in favor of frozen ones; and added blueberries for extra nutrients and fiber. The classic combination of blueberries and peaches makes this ooey-gooey cobbler a summertime favorite.

SERVES 4

COBBLER:

Nonstick cooking spray

3 cups frozen sliced peaches, thawed and coarsely chopped

1 cup frozen blueberries, thawed

½ cup small tapioca pearls

Juice and finely grated zest of 1 lemon

2 tablespoons agave nectar

½ teaspoon ground ginger

¼ teaspoon ground cinnamon

¼ teaspoon salt

TOPPING:

½ cup rolled oats (not instant)

¼ cup almond flour

2 tablespoons coarsely ground flaxseed

¼ cup frozen apple juice concentrate, thawed

2 tablespoons light butter, such as Land O'Lakes, melted

FOR SERVING:

¾ cup plain nonfat Greek yogurt

1 whole vanilla bean, split and scraped

1 teaspoon agave nectar

Preheat the oven to 350°F. Spray four (6-ounce) ramekin dishes with cooking spray. Set aside.

In a mixing bowl, combine the peaches, blueberries, tapioca, lemon juice and zest, agave nectar, ginger, cinnamon, and salt. Using a rubber spatula, toss the peach mixture together until all of the ingredients are evenly distributed. Set aside.

To make the topping, in a separate bowl combine the oats, flour, and flaxseed. Pour in the apple juice and melted butter and mix with a fork to form a coarse meal.

Divide the fruit mixture among the prepared ramekins, filling to just below the rim. Gently pat the topping over the fruit to cover completely. Put the ramekins on a rimmed baking pan. Bake until the juices bubble up and the crust is golden brown, 15 to 17 minutes.

To make the yogurt topping for serving, in a small bowl combine the yogurt, vanilla bean, and agave nectar. Mix with a spoon until well blended.

Serve the mini-cobblers in the ramekins topped with a dollop of vanilla yogurt.

Per serving: 380 calories, 9 g total fat (1 g saturated), 3 mg cholesterol, 217 mg sodium, 10 g protein, 6 g fiber, 71 g carb

Lighter Lemon Bars

Lemon bars are one of those treats that always seem to be the first to go at a potluck or cookie swap—there's always that one neighbor with the "perfect recipe." Most lemon bars start off with a thick base of buttery shortbread that's layered with lemon custard made with egg yolks. This lightened-up version has a thin, flaky crust topped with a velvety, airy custard made from whipped egg whites combined with freshly squeezed lemon juice and zest. Moist, zingy, and beautifully garnished with a snowy dusting of powdered sugar, these bright, refreshing bars will make you the belle of the ball at the next neighborhood gathering.

MAKES 8 BARS

CRUST:

Nonstick cooking spray

1 cup all-purpose flour

½ cup powdered sugar, plus more for dusting

½ teaspoon baking powder

¼ teaspoon salt

3 tablespoons light butter, such as Land O'Lakes, cold and cut into small cubes

2 tablespoons ice water

FILLING:

4 large egg whites

1 large egg

½ cup freshly squeezed lemon juice (from 2 large lemons)

2 teaspoons finely grated lemon zest

1 cup granulated sugar

1 tablespoon whole wheat flour

To make the crust, preheat the oven to 350°F. Line an 8-by-8-inch square baking pan with parchment paper, allowing the excess to hang over the sides. Coat with nonstick spray.

In a mixing bowl, sift together the flour, powdered sugar, baking powder, and salt. Cut in the butter with a fork until a coarse meal forms. Sprinkle with the ice water and mix just until the dough forms a ball. Gather the dough into a ball, cover with plastic wrap, and refrigerate for 15 minutes.

When the dough has chilled, press an even layer into the prepared baking pan. Bake for 10 minutes, until the crust is firm to the touch.

To make the filling, in a mixing bowl combine the egg whites, egg, lemon juice, and zest. Using a handheld electric mixer, beat on medium speed until well combined. Sprinkle in the sugar and flour. Continue to beat until smooth and thick.

Pour the lemon filling evenly over the hot crust and smooth the surface with a rubber spatula. Bake for 20 minutes, until firm and the edges start to pull away from the sides of the pan.

Let the lemon bars cool completely in the pan, about 1 hour. Cut into bars and dust with powdered sugar before serving.

Per serving: 227 calories, 3 g total fat (1 g saturated), 25 mg cholesterol, 174 mg sodium, 4 g protein, 1 g fiber, 47 g carb

Chocolate Chip Cookies

Chocolate chip cookies may just be the most beloved cookie in the country, not to mention the undoing of many healthy eaters. This chocolate chip cookie rehab uses date puree to give moisture to the cookies without any added fat. Made from cooked dates and water, date puree can be substituted one-for-one in place of oil or butter fat in most dessert recipes. Unsweetened cocoa powder, egg whites, whole wheat flour, and just a half a cup of mini chocolate chips come together to create a soft, chewy, and low-fat chocolate chip cookie with a nicely crisped outer edge. Store cookies in an airtight container for up to two days.

MAKES 16 COOKIES

Nonstick cooking spray

4 ounces pitted dates (1 cup)

½ cup water

1 teaspoon pure vanilla extract

¼ cup light brown sugar, packed

¼ cup granulated sugar

2 large egg whites

½ cup all-purpose flour

½ cup whole wheat flour

½ teaspoon baking powder

Pinch salt

½ cup mini chocolate chips

Preheat the oven to 375°F. Coat two cookie sheets with nonstick cooking spray.

To make the date puree, combine the dates and water in a microwave-safe dish and cover with plastic wrap. Cook on high until the dates are very soft, about 5 minutes. Check and stir the dates every minute. Drain the dates and put them into a food processor. Add the vanilla and puree until smooth. You should have about ½ cup.

Scrape the date puree into a mixing bowl. Add the brown and granulated sugars. Using a handheld electric mixer, beat the dates and sugars on medium-low speed until creamy. Add the egg white and continue to beat until no grains of sugar remain, about 4 minutes.

In a separate bowl, combine the flours, baking powder, and salt. Using a rubber spatula, mix in the creamed date-and-sugar mixture, blending gently but thoroughly until a batter forms. Fold in the chocolate chips.

Drop the dough by tablespoonful onto the prepared cookie sheets. Bake until the edges of the cookies are golden brown, about 7 minutes. Cool in the pan for 5 minutes, then transfer to a wire rack to cool completely.

Per serving (2 cookies): 205 calories, 4 g total fat (2 g saturated), 0 mg cholesterol, 85 mg sodium, 4 g protein, 3 g fiber, 43 g carb

Rice Pudding with Raisins

Humble rice pudding has all of the things you're looking for in a comfort food—the sweet, milky concoction is creamy and satisfying, with just a touch of cinnamon and spice. Some homemade batches use sweetened condensed milk, heavy cream, and whole eggs, which add a tremendous amount of calories and artery-clogging saturated fat. This rehabbed version starts out with brown rice, which imparts a sweet, nutty flavor that's a perfect base for this dessert. Briefly simmering low-fat milk with vanilla and orange zest infuses intense flavor that permeates this aromatic pudding. The result is a grown-up and much healthier reimagining of a childhood favorite.

SERVES 8

4 cups low-fat milk

¼ teaspoon salt

1 cinnamon stick

2 strips orange zest

1 vanilla bean

3 cups cooked brown rice

¼ cup sugar

½ cup raisins

1 teaspoon ground cinnamon, for dusting

Pour the milk into a large pot and put over medium heat. Add the salt, cinnamon stick, and orange zest. Using a paring knife, split the vanilla bean down the middle lengthwise, scrape out the seeds, and add them to the pot; add the empty pod as well. Cover and simmer for 5 minutes.

Uncover the pot, stir in the rice, and let the milk return to a simmer. When it boils, give it a stir and add the sugar. Cook and stir for 15 minutes over a medium-low flame, until the mixture is creamy and starts to thicken. (The pudding will continue to firm up as it cools.)

Reduce the heat to low. Remove the cinnamon stick, zest, and vanilla bean. Fold in the raisins and continue to cook for another 5 minutes, until the raisins are plump. Spoon the pudding into a serving dish and dust with the ground cinnamon. Serve chilled or at room temperature.

Per serving: 186 calories, 2 g total fat (1 g saturated), 6 mg cholesterol, 128 mg sodium, 6 g protein, 2 g fiber, 37 g carb

Chocolate Orange Biscotti

Biscotti are twice-baked, crispy Italian cookies that are often served as a light dessert with coffee. The sticky dough is first shaped into a log and baked until firm, then sliced and baked again to draw out the moisture and create the perfect crunch. Flecked with citrusy orange zest and bittersweet chocolate chips, these biscotti contain hardly any fat and come in at fewer than 150 calories for two cookies. Once completely cooled, the biscotti can be stored in an airtight container for up to 2 weeks.

MAKES 24 BISCOTTI

1½ cups all-purpose flour

1¼ teaspoons baking powder

¼ teaspoon salt

2 tablespoons light butter, such as Land O'Lakes, at room temperature

¾ cup sugar

1 teaspoon pure anise or vanilla extract

1 large egg

2 large egg whites, divided

¼ cup mini semisweet chocolate chips

¼ cup chopped orange zest

Preheat the oven to 350°F. Line a baking pan with parchment paper.

Sift the flour, baking powder, and salt together in a small bowl. In a mixing bowl, using a handheld electric mixer, cream together the butter, sugar, and anise or vanilla until light and fluffy. Beat in the egg and 1 egg white. Using a rubber spatula, gradually add the flour mixture, then the chocolate chips and orange zest. Shape the dough into a log (the dough will be sticky), place on the prepared baking pan, and, using your hands, flatten out the log shape a bit.

Whisk the remaining egg white with a fork and brush over the dough. Bake for 25 minutes or until lightly browned. Remove the pan from the oven and let cool for 10 minutes. Decrease the oven temperature to 250°F.

Transfer the log to a cutting board and use a serrated knife to cut into 24 slices. Arrange the biscotti slices side by side in the same baking pan and bake for another 20 minutes, until crisp. Remove the pan from the oven and transfer the cookies to a wire rack to cool.

Allow the cookies to cool completely before serving.

Per serving (2 biscotti): 143 calories, 3 g total fat (1 g saturated), 16 mg cholesterol, 130 mg sodium, 3 g protein, 1 g fiber, 28 g carb

Acknowledgments

EVERYDAY HEALTH

Everyday Health and Trium would like to extend special thanks to author and recipe developer extraordinaire JoAnn Cianciulli for helping us create so many of the delicious recipes in this book (see page 164). We'd also like to thank Maureen Namkoong for her enormous contributions as well as editor Julie Will (and the great team at Harper Wave, including Amanda Kain and Fritz Metsch), not to mention Chad Bennett and the very good folks Populus Brands.

We'd also like to thank our amazing team at Everyday Health: Michel Ballard, Patrick Brannan, Joanna Breen, Veronica Brooks, Betsy Dunn, Courtney Failla, Lori Flynn, Steve Gordon, Mike Keriakos, Laura Klein, Lesley Marker, Kelly MacDonald, Audie Metcalf, Jennifer Perciballi, Steven Petrow, Orlando Reece, Michael Rose, Chase Rosen, Alan Shapiro, Paul Slavin, and Ben Wolin; our fabulous chefs, Tana Amen, Govind Armstrong, Jill Davie, Daniel Green, Jaden Hair, Calvin Harris, Mareya Ibrahim, Candice Kumai, Scott Leibfried, Spike Mendelsohn, Aida Mollenkamp, Byron Talbott, Jet Tila, and Laura Vitale; and finally, the incredible team at Trium: Steven Acosta, Shandy Anglin, Lori Coburn, Kelly Castillo, Eric Day, Mark Koops, Sonya Masinovsky, Mike Mihovilovich, Sheva Mokarram, Clay Murphy, Eric Peters, Troy Roe, Lucie Schwartz, Jared Tobman, and Emily Van Bergen.

JOANN CIANCIULLI

Loving what I do every day is the absolute greatest joy in my life. Writing cookbooks and producing food television form a hybrid career that I created for myself and that characterize my passion for cooking in a unique way. I can't think of anyone who's got a better job!

As a result, I'm fortunate to collaborate closely with the top talent in the culinary world. This book would not have been possible without the dedication and expertise of our team of superstar chefs: Aida, Calvin, Candice, Daniel, Govind, Jaden, Jet, Jill, Laura, Mareya, Scott, and Spike. I love working with you all.

Special thanks to Sonya Masinovsky for being my right hand on set, testing the recipes down to the last grain of salt, and for possessing such an impeccable palate. You are the best!

MAUREEN NAMKOONG, M.S., R.D.

My deepest appreciation to my staff and boss, Kelly, Sheri, Jen, Beth, Courtney, and Patrick. Without their help I'd be lost. Thank you to my amazing husband, Suk, for his love and support. Luckily, I can always count on our children, Christian, Jin, and Grace, for keeping everything in perspective. To my parents: without their support and sacrifices I certainly wouldn't be here today. Thank you!

Everyday Health would like to thank JoAnn Cianciulli for developing the following recipes:

Tropical Parfait

Grab-and-Go Bagel and Lox Sandwich

Cheesy Broccoli and Potato Scramble

Cranberry-Ginger Oatmeal

Lemon Poppy Seed Muffins

Whole Grain Waffles with Ricotta

Caramelized Onion, Bacon, and Mushroom Frittata

Creamy Kale and Artichoke Dip with Garlic Toasts

Fresh Figs Wrapped in Prosciutto with Balsamic Glaze

Grilled Sirloin Skewers with Homemade Steak Sauce

Spicy Sausage-Stuffed Mushrooms

Mini Crab Cakes with Mustard-Dill Sauce

Refried Bean Quesadilla with Guacamole Dipping Sauce

Garlicky Green Olive Hummus

Linguine with Clam Sauce

Barley Risotto with Fennel and Radicchio

Tuscan Tuna and White Bean Casserole

Thai Noodles with Peanut-Ginger Sauce

Cajun Shrimp and Grits

Penne Pasta with Roasted Garlic-Arugula Pesto

Miso Salmon

Chicken Caesar Salad

Beef Burgundy Stew

Moroccan Butternut Squash and Chickpea Tagine

Turkey Pot Pie

Sour Cream Coffee Cake

Strawberry Cheesecake

Lighter Lemon Bars

Chocolate Chip Cookies

Rice Pudding with Raisins

Chocolate Orange Biscotti

Index

Page references in *italics* refer to illustrations.

About the Authors

JOANN CIANCIULLI

JoAnn Cianciulli is the co-executive producer of *Recipe Rehab*. With more than ten years of experience, JoAnn is known as one of the food industry's top insiders and has produced countless shows, including *MasterChef* on Fox and Bravo's *Top Chef*. She is also author of nearly a dozen cookbooks, including the acclaimed *L.A.'s Original Farmers Market Cookbook*. JoAnn lives in Los Angeles, California.

MAUREEN NAMKOONG, M.S., R.D.

Maureen Namkoong is a nutritionist and registered dietician. As the director of Nutrition and Fitness at Everyday Health, Maureen manages a staff of dietitians and personal trainers that provide counseling to the members of the Everyday Health network and oversees meal plan development, recipe creation, and nutrition data integrity. She is challenged every day with bringing the best health tools, advice, and information to the Everyday Health community.